ESCAPING

an

Evolutionary

Dead-End

Wavell F. Cowan

To my grandchildren

*with my hope they will experience the
beginnings of a new evolutionary path*

With Thanks.
An author needs an editor.
Fortunately I have had two:
Brett Bonanny and Earline Marsh

Also a book needs critical readers.
Again I've had two:
Derek Page and Tom Allen

The front cover design speaks eloquently
to this book's content. The title
"Escaping an Evolutionary Dead-End",
promises not only a discussion of why
something is seriously amiss with the manner
in which our societies are presently evolving,
but also what steps are needed to escape
from this unsatisfactory trajectory.

The background of a star-studded night sky
reinforces the evolutionary context within which
the subject matter is to be treated. For it is the
night sky that has provided the evidence upon
which science has built a coherent picture of the
evolutionary past that inexorably has brought
us to the world we are experiencing today.

For the thousands of years of our existence as a species, information flowing from the night sky has been evident to us as a twinkling myriad of stars sweeping in great arcs across the heavens – a backdrop to the wandering lights of our own planetary system. This inspired our earliest imaginings and contributed to the creation of our myths and religions.

In modern times with the aid of powerful telescopes and sophisticated sensors, this information has taken on new meaning. Interpreted now according to the laws of physics and the gravitational equations first advanced by Einstein, these observations reveal a picture of events associated with an expanding universe.

Tracing this scientific logic backwards in time we follow a contracting universe that billions of years ago shrinks to a giant fireball in which temperatures are so high matter cannot exist. A sea of energy pervades this early universe. High frequency random interactions prevent photons of light from traveling any distance undisturbed. Only with subsequent expansion and cooling – some 13.7 billion years ago – did the temperatures in the universe fall to a level at which energy could coalesce into matter. Protons and electrons then combined to create mainly hydrogen, the simplest of elements. As perceived by Einstein's famous equation, that $E=MC^2$, huge amounts of energy disappeared for every resulting gram of matter created. This massive coalescence greatly emptied space.

Light then began an unprecedented and largely unimpeded journey throughout the universe. This "first light" is now identified as the "background radiation", the earliest observational data available to scientists.

By extrapolation of their cosmic equations further backwards in time, scientists conjecture that in the preceding quarter billion or so years, a sea of energy inflated mightily from a colossal explosion emanating from a point source. This beginning is now commonly referred to as the "Big Bang". Thus, as conceived today, began the space/time experiment of our universe.

From the moment of first light, according to modern cosmology, matter driven by gravitational and inertial properties, gradually coalesced into galaxies and stars. Fusion, occurring within stars over their lifetimes, forged new and heavier elements. When the accelerating fusion within such stars repeatedly ended their lives in novas and supernovas, space became seeded with new elements of the periodic table. These elements became the building blocks for creating new molecules of ever-greater complexity.

This progression of new star formation came to include planetary systems. On at least one such planet formed in our solar system some 4.5 billion years ago, conditions were ripe for initiating what became a massive increase in complex carbon-based molecules. This ultimately led to a complexity that achieved the self-reproducing capability we have come to identify as "life".

So was initiated a new evolutionary track whereby molecular evolution was replaced in importance by the evolution of organisms – again of increasing complexity – but driven now by the guiding principles of Darwinian evolution. This eventually produced an oxygen atmosphere resulting in new levels of complexity, leading ultimately to the development of consciousness as an attribute of a new species, *Homo Sapiens*.

So began yet another evolutionary path, now driven by the ability of consciousness in a new species to drive consequences in a process called civilization. The new conceptualization and communication skills associated with consciousness slowly achieved the new inventions and practices that became evolutionary stepping-stones.

Thus did our species advance from tribal hunters and gatherers to urban farmers and herders to inhabitants of early cit-

ies and nations. Then occurred the rise of science, the industrial revolution it inspired, and now the world that we, living
today, are experiencing.

Philosophically then, we represent the current location on
a relatively new evolutionary path, continuing a process initiated by the Big Bang. The fact that our bodies are constructed
from basic elements forged in the fiery hearts of ancient stars
is an ever-present reminder of this connection.

The evolution of consciousness has now replaced Darwinian evolution in importance. This means that the evolutionary
path determining the future of our species no longer depends
primarily on chance genetic mutations. Rather it now depends
on the consequences of actions flowing from the collective
consciousness of our species.

Overwhelmingly our daily activities are no longer occupied
in producing what we need to sustain our individual lives and
satisfy our particular wants. Our working lives embedded in
the societies in which we live, contribute through the economic system to the overall availability of a vast array of goods
and services. These, through the purchase mechanism, now
provide for most of our needs and wants. Daily, our lives are
now supported by the largely anonymous labors of countless
individuals, both past and present. Their participation in the
economic system has or is presently contributing to the wellbeing of each and every one of us. Thus it is to the effective
organization of our societies that we now depend for our survival and wellbeing.

When we come into existence, we contribute to the consciousness of our societies and species for a brief moment in our evolutionary journey. In this sense we are the latest participants in the ongoing evolutionary process that determines our future destiny as a species. Each of us, in making a living for ourselves, necessarily contributes in some manner to the survival or wellbeing of others.

In large part, the nature of the societies we enter determines the contribution we are likely to make to this common welfare. In this regard the historical record is clear. Those modern societies that have best supported the opportunity for their citizens through education, to individually find their "best place" in the economic system and the means therein to maximize their productivity are the societies that have most prospered. How well these outcomes are achieved is an important measure of evolutionary progress. This connection has many ramifications.

It means, for instance, to the extent that people are poor or unemployed or underemployed or under-educated, or unhealthy, or imprisoned, or otherwise wards of the state, or engaged in activities that are damaging to our present or future capabilities to perform most productively, are all measures of lost productivity, greatly diminishing the prosperity of all and thus impeding our evolutionary progress.

Our continuing inability to alleviate these characteristic defects in our current societies in any significant way has created the widespread feelings of discontent to which the recent "Occupy Wall Street" contagion and the "Tea Party" movement are somewhat blindly responding.

The evidence offered by current outcomes in dealing with problems important to societal progress – the workings of the economy, the growing gap between the few that are rich and the many that are not, the failures of the wars on drugs and poverty, the educational deficits in the labor force, the obesity level in the population at large, etc. – all these suggest that the approaches we are taking as a society to counter such defects may well be fundamentally flawed. Ongoing failures of this nature are impediments to the successful evolution of our species, even though we may think of them in far more parochial terms.

In this book I explore the likelihood that these failures are a consequence of the manner in which our societies typically tackle such problems. These approaches have evolved based on historical circumstances that no longer persist. We have been following an evolutionary path that has served us reasonably well. Now, in our fast paced, high-tech world, new and different circumstances have arisen. These make feasible new approaches that bring into question the current means by which our societies seek to advance their wellbeing. In effect, our current path may well be leading us into a blind canyon, an evolutionary dead-end.

How might we escape from this dead-end pathway? Historical evidence associates three fundamental concepts with successful problem solving. These concepts are, however, conspicuously absent in the problem solving approaches our societies typically adopt. Appreciating this, and taking actions in accordance with these concepts, could offer the means to improve on current, unsatisfactory outcomes. Doing so would help us escape from our current evolutionary path by reshaping practices, which, if allowed to continue unchecked, could plausibly endanger the very survival of our species.

This book is not an academic study replete with footnotes. Rather it describes a personal journey, the outcome of a long and thoughtful enquiry into the underlying significance of my own practical experiences over an unusual "problem solving" lifetime. These have been derived from my professional career as a scientist, inventor, entrepreneur and businessman and from involvements in local community groups and other organizations.

Practical reality is a great teacher. So my approach in this book is to recount the stories that flow from such practical lifetime experiences. In this way I hope to better illuminate the importance of the three concepts referred to above. This effort occupies the first part of this book.

A follow-along is to show how these three concepts if incorporated into our thinking could alter the approaches taken to alleviate the defects currently impeding societal progress. Events in my own life's journey have provided experiences that bear on such questions. These stories provide a conceptual perspective on how important contemporary problems could be tackled, in sharp contrast to present practices.

Attention is thereby directed to new approaches of a form that ultimately out of necessity, I believe, will emerge. These could dramatically alter the course of our evolutionary path allowing us to escape the dead end that mounting evidence informs is our current destination as a species. These stories occupy the second part of this book.

I have given much thought over the years to these perspectives. This has been accompanied by much reading in contemporary journals and magazines dealing with business, the economy, and current events over the past 55 years. Once the above perspectives were uppermost in my mind, it was surprising how much evidence could be adduced from such general reading to support their validity. On the other hand, I have yet to find persuasive evidence that they are misguided. My hope is that readers, when engaging with these perspectives, will not simply dismiss them out-of-hand in the belief that current "expert" opinion cannot be wrong. History unequivocally teaches quite the opposite.

Assembling this intellectual autobiography, a task stretching over many years, has been difficult but enjoyable. Perhaps the outcome will contribute something of value from my own brief moment at the current frontier of our evolutionary journey begun so many billions of years ago.

Contents

Concepts

Chapter I

Science

The philosopher Francis Bacon served both as Attorney General and then Lord Chancellor of England at the turn of the 17th century. He was born 18 years after Copernicus' deathbed publication of his mathematical treatise based on a sun-centered solar system. He died just 17 years before the birth of Isaac Newton. He was a contemporary of Galileo, also of Kepler, Gilbert, and Harvey, and was aware of their early contributions to modern science. Thus Francis Bacon lived at an interesting time – the dawn of the scientific age. Quite remarkably, he recognized this. In his *Novum Organum* published a few years before his death in 1626, he expounded on a new way of thinking.

In his words ...

"There are and can be only two ways of searching into and discovering truth. The one flies from the senses and particulars to the most general axioms, and from these principles, the truth of which it takes for settled and immovable, proceeds to judgment and to the discovery of middle axioms. And this way is now in fashion.

The other derives axioms from the senses and particulars, rising by a gradual and unbroken ascent, so that it arrives at the most general axioms last of all. This is the true way, but as yet untried.

Therefore from a closer and purer league between these two faculties, the experimental and the rational (such as has never yet been made), much may be hoped."

Thus did Bacon provide the earliest description of what has come to be known as the scientific method.

What caught my interest was Bacon's notion that scientific thinking was very different from the normal way of thinking prevalent in his day. In reading Bacon's description and characterization of this "old way" of thinking, it seemed clear to me that with a bit of language updating it was an accurate description of much of what is commonly heard today. I began to wonder about this. If scientific thinking is, today, still different from the norm what exactly does that mean?

For most of my adult life I have been a practicing professional scientist. Yet until some dozen years ago, I hadn't given any real thought as to how exactly I went about my activity nor why I chose to do it in that particular way.

After much thought, I have reached the conclusion that I came to function as a scientist not by being taught – here's how you need to "think" in order to become a scientist – but rather as a consequence of a great deal of practice and experience that most people are simply never exposed to.

The scientific method as expressed by Bacon, "... *a closer and purer league between the experimental and the rational* ..." is typically taught today in elementary and high school science courses. Scientific thought is driven by experimentation. Scientific ideas are tested by experiments and they are sustained only so long as no experimental data is found to deny them. These, so to speak, are the rules of the game, but they don't explain how best to play the game.

I learned to play the game as a consequence of my experiences throughout graduate school and my subsequent scientific career in the same way that anybody learns to play a game well – by a great deal of practice with perhaps the help of a coach. Much of what happens is really training your body to respond automatically in ways that make you a better player. Think of how one skates in hockey, swings a club in golf, or a racket in tennis. Your body has to know how to do it without your thinking about it. In fact when you try and do so is typically when you play your worst. Comparably, the practice of science sets in place patterns of thought that become instinctive, just as the practice of a golf swing makes it instinctive.

After long reflection, I have concluded that what I absorbed by practice and experience were two skills and two attributes that I believe explain how I think and function as a scientist.

I attended graduate school at the *Institute of Paper Chemistry* in Appleton, Wisconsin. This school was established in the mid 1930s by a group of far-sighted paper mill executives. It was to be financed by the paper industry to train scientists who would become available for the future benefit of their Industry. When I attended some twenty years later, the primary responsibility of the professors was to teach. The student body was small, some five to ten entering annually. The result, compared to many graduate schools, was an unusual connection of all students not only with all professors but also with all the doctoral students and their projects. The first two years of lectures and labs familiarized us with all the many branches of science that are important to an understanding of the materials and processes employed in the manufacture of pulp and paper. This period included a master's research project developed by each student with some professorial support. Successful completion of the master's program allowed a student to enter a very unusual program to qualify for doctoral candidacy.

Each student was given a problem associated in one way or another with pulp and/or papermaking. In a 4-6 week period the project required researching the problem and producing a report on a proposed experimental program that would make a significant advance toward an answer, as well as providing the background information supporting this particular approach. This report was defended in an oral presentation before a faculty board. A successful outcome produced another problem of a different nature, with the same requirement. A final problem then had to be proposed by the student and similarly executed. Surviving this four-month trial by fire allowed a student to propose a subject for a doctoral thesis. This essentially meant doing the same thing once again, this time satisfying a thesis committee that the scope of the work and its probable outcome were persuasive as a subject for a doctoral thesis.

The repetitive practice required by this graduate school program developed two skills. First, was the manner of researching a problem in order to get a "feel for it." The second was "seeing" how a particular experimental program could best answer currently unanswerable questions. Both of these skills expanded on the already substantial knowledge base acquired by the labs and lectures of the master's program. The difficulty is explaining what is meant by "getting a feel" for a problem, and what is meant by "seeing" a beneficial experimental program.

Before attempting to clarify these concepts I'd like to make a diversion by introducing ideas sourced in my readings from the history and philosophy of science. These ideas resonated strongly in relation to my own scientific work.

The first is from Thomas Kuhn's 1962 publication, *The Structure of Scientific Revolutions*. Kuhn identified the constraining consequences of the normal path by which scientists come to be trained. They are taken to a frontier of knowledge embedded in the minds of their professors, and, for their doctorate, they work closely under the influence of some particular professor. Therefore, according to Kuhn, science at any time *"is predicated on the assumption that the scientific community knows what the world is like . . . and often suppresses fundamental novelties because they are necessarily subversive of its basic commitments."*

Kuhn's point is that major scientific advances do not occur in a uniform cumulative manner with every building block being elevated by a prior one in a systematic and predictable manner. Instead, such advances occur in discontinuous and uncertain periods of dramatic change when an anomaly *"subverts the existing tradition of scientific practice."* In other words, only rarely can a person break away from the standard scientific path that has reliably led to a PhD. Kuhn describes such departures from the norm as scientific revolutions — *"the tradition-shattering complements to the tradition-bound activity of normal science."*

What resonated with me from Kuhn's work was the importance, with respect to my own scientific career, of my graduate school training having been so different from the normal path Kuhn described. The school I attended gave a great deal of latitude to its students. I was allowed to follow my own nose, to explore topics largely on my own. The adventures that attended my doctoral thesis work were a direct consequence of this.

For my thesis I proposed to determine how the pore structure of wet fiber mats affected the manner in which the mat dried when placed on a heated surface. This involved measuring the heat and mass transfer consequences of drying wet fiber mats with differing pore structures. The experimental techniques I proposed were largely based on those employed a few years earlier by previous students. My proposed approach to analysis mirrored mathematical procedures my future thesis chairman had developed in related work. The novelty of the outcome and the solid base from which it was to be achieved led to its acceptance as a viable doctoral thesis proposal.

Some six months into the project, after perfecting apparatus, etc. I began generating very peculiar data. I ultimately realized and then demonstrated that this was due to flaws in the experimental techniques I had inherited. This unfortunate fact had been obscured from my predecessors because their experiments had employed process rates substantially higher than mine and the defect only became obvious at my lower rates. This blew a big hole in my thesis plans. I couldn't proceed without resolving it.

Fortunately, in talking about the problem with a friendly professor unconnected with my project, he made a suggestion, which, after considerable effort, I was able to develop into a successful technique. This work occupied a substantial period of time and included some rather sleepless nights. Thereafter data production was rapid. The data was reproducible, logical and esthetically pleasing. However, I ran into trouble with the detailed mathematical logic of the complex heat and mass flow data that I had generated. The only apparent resolution to this problem meant that the prior mathematical work of my thesis chairman was seriously flawed. After more sleepless nights I found no recourse but to broach this difficult question with him. Our subsequent debate failed to achieve a resolution and left me in limbo. Fortunately, my thesis chairman, a chemical engineer, was sufficiently humble to suggest that we consult the chairman of the mathematics department at a neighboring university. This consultation convincingly supported the validity of my resolution of the problem and so cleared the air for completing a successful piece of work.

Such failure episodes as those I have described are highly unlikely to occur when working closely with a professor who has spent years focused on the area of research that the doctoral student is engaged with.

I now appreciate that these two, at the time quite traumatic events, heavily influenced my subsequent thinking as a scientist. Since then I have never approached any problem without an instinctive skepticism and willingness to disbelieve. This, I am now convinced, is an attribute of fundamental importance to the way I think as a scientist.

A second author, whose work resonated with me, is that of the philosopher Karl Popper in his 1934 publication, *The Logic of Scientific Discovery.*

In Popper's words . . .

"It is easy to obtain confirmations, or verifications, for nearly every theory – if we look for confirmations. Confirmations should count only if they are the result of risky predictions; that is to say, if, unenlightened by the theory in question, we should have expected an event which was incompatible with the theory – an event which would have refuted the theory.

Every "good" scientific theory is a prohibition: it forbids certain things to happen. The more a theory forbids, the better it is. A theory which is not refutable by any conceivable event is non-scientific. Irrefutability is not a virtue of a theory (as people often think) but a vice. Every genuine test of a theory is an attempt to falsify it, or to refute it. Testability is falsifiability; but there are degrees of testability: some theories are more testable, more exposed to refutation, than others; they take, as it were, greater risks. Confirming evidence should not count except when it is the result of a genuine test of the theory; and this means that it can be presented as a serious but unsuccessful attempt to falsify the theory. Some genuinely testable theories, when found to be false, are still upheld by their admirers – for example by introducing ad hoc some auxiliary assumption, or by reinterpreting the theory ad hoc in such a way that it escapes refutation. Such a procedure is always possible, but it rescues the theory from refutation only at the price of destroying, or at least lowering, its scientific status. One can sum up all this by saying that the criterion of the scientific status of a theory is its falsifiability, or refutability, or testability."

This view of science, I realized, exactly fit the way I came to pursue my own scientific activities. Obtaining unexpected data or outcomes means the current way of looking at a problem is flawed. Acknowledging this fact has been the launch point for many of my successful projects. This required a willingness, once satisfied that particular data were reliable, to accept that my thinking had to change. Recognizing scientific work as a continuous search to find evidence that proves current thinking wrong or incomplete is an essential attribute for good scientific work. The philosopher Alfred North Whitehead similarly stressed the importance of *"irreducible and stubborn facts"* in guiding scientific thought.

Those who can function most successfully as scientists fully accept that scientific endeavor can never prove any idea to be true. They recognize its sole purpose is to seek proof that something currently believed, is untrue. They appreciate that scientific thinking is the most effective means of solving problems and developing useful knowledge. Thus, scientific "truth" is a philosophic notion, an act of faith. It is irrelevant to scientific endeavor itself, which is best described as a search to prove that a current belief is, in fact, untrue.

I would like now to place into one context the concept of the two skills required to support scientific thinking – getting a "feel" for a problem and "seeing" a beneficial experimental program – and also the concept of the two attributes important to effective scientific thinking – having a willingness to disbelieve, and having a dedication to the search to disprove as the means to strengthen or abandon ideas.

Consider that, metaphorically, we live on a surface at the top of an inverted pyramid. On this surface our senses provide us with the inputs that our brains convert to the images we live by – all that we know but cannot fully understand. Journeys of the mind, penetrating downward into the inverted pyramid, are needed to seek out ideas that can connect disparate surface observations into the meaningful patterns that explain and create understanding. The more deeply such journeys penetrate, the more encompassing are the ideas and the connections that can be made from them.

The first skill needed to support scientific thinking deals with the process of following, in this journey of the mind, all the clues one can find in a good library. During my time in graduate school I enjoyed the use of the best pulp and paper science library in the world. An early concern that written reports and oral examinations might reveal embarrassing omissions in my work drove me to pursue as thoroughly as possible all such clues. Later came the attribute of having the open mind encouraged by an instinctive skepticism of current belief, a willingness to pursue obscure paths rather than to cling to the most obvious.

In terms of my analogy, this attribute encourages one to penetrate further downward into the inverted pyramid and thus to see connections that might otherwise not be perceived. In all of the many journeys of the mind that have occupied my life as a scientist, I have always arrived at a time when for unexplainable reasons I suddenly "see" a new pattern of connections that resonates, that proclaims, "Here is the proper way to go."

Arriving at that point is quite frankly an act of faith. I believe I will arrive at that point sometime and that I will know when I have arrived there.

This is what I mean by "getting a feel" for a problem.

At this point one needs to develop an experimental program to explore this "proper way to go." Here, one must conceive the form of the experiments that will illuminate and demonstrate the value of the ideas that collectively have indicated the proper way to go. This means identifying all the measurements needed to try and disprove the idea being investigated.

One needs to think of all the possible scenarios that could be offered in disputing the validity of the approach under investigation. Making sure that all such possible refutations have been identified ensures that the experimental program and the measurements it employs will offer the maximum opportunity to discourage the idea – or conversely of course to support it.

That's what Karl Popper meant: *"It is easy to obtain confirmations, or verifications, for nearly every theory – if we look for confirmations. Confirmations should count only if they are the result of risky predictions".*

The quality of the outcome of the journeys of the mind I have described requires the necessary background and skill that allows the mind to journey deeply into the inverted pyramid and to "feel" the idea worth pursuing. Additional skill and background is needed to "find" the program of measurement that can properly test out the quality of such an idea. Without the two attributes, the skeptical mind and a focus on disproving the validity of the idea in question, any outcome will be much diminished. Attaining these skills and attributes is the consequence of much study and much practice. It is then aided or restricted by one's subsequent experiences.

Which leads to a final story.

I have emphasized the importance of my unusual graduate school experiences with how I came to function as a scientist. Of equal importance is what happened next.

When the light at the end of the tunnel of my graduate school experiences became evident, I began to think, what next? Ultimately, I was to join the Montreal engineering consulting firm owned by my father and uncle. However, I decided that a few years out in the real world was a desirable prelude to this eventual career. With this idea in mind I sent a résumé to all the paper mills in the United Kingdom seeking a job in some technical capacity.

I subsequently learned that the managing director of a paper mill in Scotland was shortly to be visiting the Institute. In view of my interest in working overseas, I approached the administration about the possibility of meeting this gentleman. The word came back that since Stanley Smith, the gentleman in question, was to be staying overnight in Appleton, he would be happy for me to pay an evening visit to his hotel room.

This meeting took place, and in due course Mr. Smith explained that he had only recently taken over at Clyde Paper Company in Glasgow with the intention of straightening out a mill that had become mired in serious financial difficulties. At the end of the meeting he casually mentioned that he was looking for a new technical manager for the mill and would be considering my application as for that job. Without the least hesitation I replied that if he offered me the job I would certainly accept it.

As you can now readily guess, Stanley Smith did offer me this job, and, on the basis of a three to five year commitment, I accepted. And so fresh out of graduate school I took up a senior management position in a Scottish paper mill. To achieve such responsibilities and authority immediately out of university with virtually no intermediary experience was unusual. I was too young and inexperienced to recognize this at the time. I saw the job only as an exciting opportunity to use my now extensive technical knowledge and freshly honed research skills in a practical way. It turned out that these resources and my youthful confidence in their suitability proved adequate to the task.

On arriving at Clyde Paper Company I faced an array of serious technical problems and a demoralized, ineffective technical staff. Tackling every problem just as I had at graduate school – that is, seeking to understand basic root causes of problems by intensive study and thought, followed by ensuring careful and efficient experimentation – worked successfully time and again. I built up a highly effective, problem solving, technical group that I later realized was unusual in composition and organization when compared to industry norms.

Early successes gave me a free hand in technical matters at the mill. Also my senior position and the support of the managing director gave me great authority to get things done. These circumstances allowed me to acquire, in three exciting and highly productive years, the equivalent of at least a dozen years experience in any normal career path. This fact, after my return to Canada and a brief-but-unhappy stay at my father's engineering firm, gave me the confidence to start my own business as a research and development specialist in the paper industry.

I then began to observe that the normal way paper mills went about problem solving was very different from what I had become accustomed to. It was a far more superficial and empirical approach – much more trial and error based – in which doing something quickly was of the essence. This allowed no time for seriously thinking a problem through. I was able to capitalize on this to the benefit of my consulting business.

In retrospect, I realized that the only thing that had made it possible for me to have had the opportunity to "try out" in an industrial environment the same approaches I'd learned at graduate school, to have as it were a seamless transition from graduate school to Industry, was the incredibly unlikely fact that my first real job in Industry was as the boss.

In other words, it was a quite unique graduate school experience that imbedded in me the two attributes that I feel are so important to good scientific work. Also, it was the unusual amount of practice I received at graduate school that allowed me to develop the two skills needed to creatively research problems and effectively test the validity of conceived solutions. Further, without the unique circumstances of my early employment, I probably would never have had the opportunity to carry my graduate school experiences directly into the commercial environment and thus establish them, unknowingly, as fundamental to the way I functioned as a scientist.

My description of scientific thinking to this point has

emerged from a serious retrospective examination of my own life as a scientist. It does, I feel, support my earlier contention that Francis Bacon's assertion of a new way of thinking, what we now call scientific thinking, is in many ways still a new way of thinking. I have found that many people I have known, who work in the fields of science and technology, while having a measure of the practical skills I have described, frequently do not exhibit a strong commitment to the "attributes" either of "disbelieving" or of seeking to "disprove" as the primary driving force behind their activities.

Outside of the fields of science and technology, I have rarely observed the skills and attributes of scientific thinking. This is particularly evident in political discourse concerning the societal problems identified in the prologue to this book. In these areas, legislative proposals are offered with no apparent recognition that they are social "experiments". This is reflected in the manner in which they are developed and debated. The benefits to be gained by the experiment are never presented as concrete predictions based on carefully established, well-defined measurements. No time period is suggested as to when predicted outcomes should be assessed as the basis for determining the success or failure of the experiment.

The development of technology made possible by the scientific way of thinking has been the driving force for the evolutionary advances of the past few hundred years. These are reflected in the greatly enhanced possibilities for longer, healthier lives, and more diverse and attractive life opportunities.

This new evolutionary pathway was initiated at the time of Francis Bacon early in the 17th century. Previous discoveries of a scientific nature were based on unusually perceptive observations and intuitions, but not as the outcome of controlled experimentation based on scientific thinking as it was introduced by Galileo and comparably pursued to this day. Since Bacon's time, the work of a relatively small number of individuals who mastered the scientific way of thinking has been responsible for the new knowledge that has driven advances along this new evolutionary pathway. In a few hundred years this has allowed humanity to advance itself well beyond anything even remotely conceivable over the prior thousands of years of our evolutionary history.

That scientific thinking has been the basis for this remarkable progress poses a seemingly obvious question. If this is so, why do we so rarely observe the application of scientific thinking to problem solving in the critical areas that impede societal progress? Why does the political discourse concerning such problems as education, the economy, health care, the environment, etc., illustrate what Francis Bacon described as *"the old way of thinking"?*

I have indicated the extent to which I believe that chance rather than careful planning was crucial to my acquisition, unrecognized at the time, of what I now identify as "scientific thinking". I was fortunate to experience environments conducive to acquiring the skills underpinning scientific work. This made possible the events that embedded what I have called scientific "attributes" as a fundamental component of my scientific thinking. It was as if I was born to think in the old way, and only through a series of unusual life experiences did I unwittingly come to think in Bacon's new way.

Thinking along these lines suggests that brain development in response to Darwinian forces of evolution would have had no particular reason to enhance neural connections favoring anything beyond primary responses to sensory experiences; i.e. making connections important for survival. Sitting down thinking about a problem would, for most of human history, more likely have led to one being eaten by the problem rather than enhancing the likelihood of survival.

In Bacon's terms, the old way of thinking is that which is favored by the manner in which evolution has fashioned the workings of our brains. It is the "natural" way to think. The new way is alien to our species, and is, perhaps, only accessible to some unknown genetic propensities in brain structure, along with educational experiences and environments similar to those I encountered. The tentative conclusion I have reached is that the combination of the genetic propensity to think in the "old way" and the low probability that a person's educational and life experiences will alter that predisposition, explains why scientific thinking, in its modern form, was a late arrival to the human journey. This also accounts for why scientific thinking is still so poorly understood and greatly underemployed.

It seems to me, therefore, that to best make our moment in the evolution of our species a significantly more positive one, we need to create much greater awareness of the significance of Bacon's new way of thinking – the scientific way. Only then might public opinion come to better appreciate its meaning and act to encourage the legislative process to demonstrate a more scientific approach in developing legislation dealing with our fundamental societal problems.

This would mean seeing proposed legislation as experiments requiring quantitative predictions of outcomes by which their validity is to be tested. Absent this, our evolutionary journey will likely continue on its current path, possibly requiring cruel and disaster-driven adjustments before escaping from its current dead-end destination.

Chapter II

*P*luralism

*P*luralism is a word descriptive of an important idea. It can be used to distinguish a multi-pronged from a single focus approach to problem solving. The greater the number of active entities individually and separately engaged in the search for meaningful answers in respect to any field of activity or inquiry, the greater is the pluralism being exhibited. The degree of pluralism is thus a measure of the diversity of approaches that are simultaneously being pursued in the search for the best answer to a common question or problem. The degree of pluralism is high when these numbers are large, and low when they are not.

In 1939 after the outbreak of war in Europe, the most famous scientist of the time, Albert Einstein, at the urging of
three Hungarian refugee physicists, Leo Szilard, Eugene
Wigner and Edward Teller, sent a letter to President Roosevelt. In it, Einstein expressed concern that Germany had the
capacity to develop an atomic bomb and would spare no effort
to do so. The first successful splitting of the uranium atom had
been accomplished a year earlier at the *Kaiser Wilhelm Institute* in Germany. This led physicists to recognize that the new
form of energy thus achieved could be used to create a bomb
of incredible explosive power. The consequences should Germany be the first to produce such a weapon were unthinkable.
As a result, Roosevelt authorized a top-secret project of the
highest priority – to develop an atomic bomb. So was born the
Manhattan Project.

To fuel an atomic bomb it was necessary to bring together
in a controlled manner, sufficient amounts of one or other of
two recently discovered radioactive materials, uranium 235 or
plutonium, so as to initiate a chain reaction. This in turn, would
convert mass to energy at an exponentially increasing rate.
The result would be the most devastating explosive power
ever conceived by man.

Uranium 235 is a naturally occurring radioactive isotope
present as a minor constituent (some 0.7%) of stable uranium
238. Plutonium is a radioactive material produced by bom-
barding uranium with high-energy particles from an atomic
pile. The problem faced by the Manhattan project was how to
produce sufficiently concentrated amounts of either of these

radioactive materials to make possible the initiation of the chain reaction that would create an atomic explosion. This required the large-scale development of a suitable method for separating the uranium 235 isotope from natural uranium, or for creating plutonium from irradiated uranium.

The best scientific minds in these fields of study were engaged in highest priority, top-secret projects to research the means of producing the necessary purity in the radioactive materials needed to trigger an atomic bomb. Four approaches emerged.

These were: Using an atomic pile to achieve the controlled chain reaction needed to produce plutonium; or to enrich uranium 235 by means of either electromagnetic separation, gaseous diffusion separation, or thermal diffusion separation. Centrifuging was also tried, but no materials available at that time for making a centrifuge could withstand the centrifugal forces generated by the extreme rotational speeds required.

After much discussion it was acknowledged that insufficient data existed to suggest favorable odds for any of these approaches proving successful as full-scale production operations, much less to distinguish between them. The fear that Germany was probably ahead of the U.S. in fission research was palpable. Time was thus believed to be of the utmost importance. This led to the remarkable decision to proceed to build large-scale plants, simultaneously, based on all four approaches. Pluralism was the defining idea for ensuring the highest probability for a successful outcome. Allowing all four conceivable methods of developing the required amounts of fissionable material to simultaneously move ahead toward industrial production ensured that if a solution existed, it would be found in the shortest possible time.

Thus began the most improbable scientific, technical and engineering feat ever attempted. Within three years, in total secrecy, great industrial buildings and infrastructure materialized in wilderness areas at Hanford on the Columbia River in the state of Washington, at Oak Ridge in Tennessee, and at Los Alamos in New Mexico.

At Hanford was built an industrial sized graphite pile used to irradiate uranium needed to produce the plutonium required to fuel a bomb. The radioactive nature of this plant's operation required that everything be remotely operated and serviced.

At Oak Ridge were built three industrial sized buildings to house the newly developed equipment that was to produce uranium 235 of a purity to fuel a bomb, by electromagnetic separation, and/or by gaseous diffusion separation, and/or by thermal diffusion separation. In all cases it was required that laboratory apparatus developed by scientists be instantaneously scaled up by several orders of magnitude to industrial-scale production processes. It was an enormous undertaking involving the collaboration of many teams of the finest engineers, industrialists and scientists in the country.

At Los Alamos, facilities were built to house and support the scientists and engineers needed to work out how the fissionable material – either plutonium from Hanford or uranium 235 from Oak Ridge – were to be fashioned into a bomb that could be controlled to reliably explode only when and where it was desired. The basic problem was that the fissionable material had to be fashioned in such a way that it could be forced together at an instantaneous moment in time. This proximity would then create the exponential increase in neutron formation, the chain reaction that would produce the atomic explosion. The different nature of the two fissionable materials, plutonium and uranium 235 required two different approaches to bomb construction.

The plutonium was to be fashioned into a hollow sphere that could be imploded by carefully arranged and tuned external explosives. This would, in a fraction of a second, uniformly collapse the plutonium into a central core of sufficient density to ensure the onset of the chain reaction. Enriched uranium could be more easily brought to criticality by using a straightforward gun-projectile approach. Several sub critical masses of uranium 235 were propelled from special guns into a central and critical mass thereby initiating the required chain reaction.

By June of 1945 this massive undertaking had successfully produced enough plutonium for only two bombs, and sufficient enriched uranium 235 for only one bomb. This latter quantity was the result of coordinating all the separation procedures installed at Oak Ridge in various stages in order to generate, in the time available, the degree of enrichment required. Project leaders decided to prove out the more difficult plutonium bomb construction with a test explosion at the Alamogordo bombing range in southern New Mexico. In July of 1945 this was successfully conducted. This set the stage for the use of the remaining two bombs for the destructive demonstrations destined to end the Second World War. On August 6th, 1945 the enriched uranium 235 bomb was dropped on Hiroshima. Three days later, the plutonium bomb was dropped on Nagasaki.

If a more "efficient," single, best-effort approach had been applied by the Manhattan Project rather than the pluralism actually pursued, it is highly unlikely the atomic bomb would have been produced in time to affect the outcome of the Second World War.

* * *

In his book, *The Double Helix*, written some 60 years ago, James Watson presented a vivid description of the events leading up to his elucidation, in collaboration with Francis Crick, of the molecular structure of DNA. It was an exciting time. Determining DNA's structure was believed ready for a solution. Various scientists around the world were pursuing this goal. As additional incentive, it was certain that success would bring with it a Nobel Prize. The major players in this intellectual race were believed to be Maurice Wilkins and Rosalind Franklin at the University of London, and the formidable Linus Pauling at Caltech.

Ironically, the post-war blossoming of scientific interest in genetic research, in understanding the basis for how life is perpetuated, was, in part, a consequence of a reaction by scientists to the successful outcome of the Manhattan project. As the dreadful implications of the existence of the atomic bomb became evident, a considerable number of scientists chose to switch out of a field associated with death into one clearly connected to life.

By the time the young James Watson arrived at Cambridge's Cavendish Labs in 1951 on a post-doctoral scholarship, labs around the world had explored the chemical nature of chromosomes. A consensus had developed that a molecule of a particular general chemical nature, named deoxyribonucleic acid (DNA) somehow housed the genetic units of heredity (genes). X-ray crystallography, the study of X-ray diffraction patterns, had shown DNA to have an ordered structure. These studies increasingly revealed the detailed internal structure of materials, and were, therefore, highly relevant to the search for the structure of DNA.

Wilkins and Franklin at the University of London's King's College were the acknowledged experts in the field of X-ray crystallography. The second strand of relevant investigation concerned studies of the three dimensional structure of inorganic ions. This had an obvious bearing on ways in which the DNA complex could be put together.

Linus Pauling of Caltech was an expert in this field. His book *The Nature of the Chemical Bond* was an acknowledged classic.

By his own admission, James Watson's depth of knowledge in either X-ray crystallography or structural chemistry was rudimentary. The scientific lure of the "gene" brought him to Cambridge with a background in microbiology rather than in chemistry or physics. Fortunately, Watson quickly connected with Cambridge's brilliant theorist, the mercurial Francis

Crick. Watson's youthful energy and down to earth approach steadied and focused his older colleague, bringing an unusually powerful synergism to their collaboration.

An important launch point for the Watson-Crick collaboration was Pauling's recent publication of his notion that DNA had a helical structure. This he had deduced more from a common sense consideration of the simple laws of structural chemistry than from any theoretical analysis, although it was not incompatible with X-ray diffraction theory. Tinker toy models constructed according to the rules of structural chemistry were used to help visualize three-dimensional alternative structures. It was through the use of this technique that Pauling had reached his conclusions.

This kind of modeling approach appealed to Watson and it became the focus for his collaboration with Crick. Their initial foray produced a three-strand, helical model that created a brief moment of excitement before becoming an obvious embarrassment. As a result, Sir Lawrence Bragg, head of the Cavendish labs, officially requested that they give up their work on DNA and get back to other projects. Recognizing their effort had been premature and that a fresh start was needed, Crick and Watson were happy to lay low. Crick returned to his work on hemoglobin. Watson began a study of the tobacco mosaic virus, a vital component of which was nucleic acid. This became a suitable mask for his continued interest in DNA. The following year Watson acquired his own copy of Pauling's book, *The Nature of the Chemical Bond* and began serious X-ray work on the tobacco mosaic virus. He also attended conferences and kept abreast of new publications.

Two pieces of information that came to Watson's attention from such activities proved of vital importance. First, he became aware of Columbia University professor Erwin Chargaff's work on the chemistry of DNA. Chargaff found that the number of adenine molecules in all his DNA preparations was very similar to the number of thymine molecules. He also found the same relationship for guanine and cytosine molecules.

Secondly, on a visit to King's College, Maurice Wilkins informally showed him a picture of an X-ray diffraction pattern for a new three-dimensional form of DNA that occurred when its molecules were surrounded by a large amount of water. With his now greater familiarity with X-ray patterns, Watson instantly recognized the importance of the pattern. It not only provided the clearest evidence yet for the helical structure of DNA, but also produced several vital helical parameters. It was time to get back to serious modeling once again.

With renewed enthusiasm, Crick and Watson convinced Sir Lawrence, that with a focused effort, Cavendish labs could win the honors for describing the structure of DNA. The final push was on. Watson favored the double helical strands, and these were constructed in the general form dictated by the Wilkin's X-ray pattern. This set the stage for the discovery, prompted by Chargaff's adenine-thymine (A-T) and guanine-cytosine (G-C) observations, that A-T and G-C base pairs had similar shapes. Modeling work then revealed that these shapes fitted very well in bridging the space between the two helical strands. Crick applied these careful measurements to his mathematical models. This provided convincing evidence for the internal consistency of the proposed model. The double helix had been elucidated. The Nobel Prize followed.

That such an unlikely duo as the mercurial and unpredictable Francis Crick and the unknown, gangly young American post-doctoral student, James Watson, should be the ones to beat the well known and eminently qualified Linus Pauling or Maurice Wilkins and Rosalind Franklin to this great prize was the improbable outcome of the pluralism that is so characteristic of scientific endeavors.

Scientific problems in any area tend to intrigue many scientists and attract their active efforts. In this sense, the activity of scientific investigation is highly inefficient in the same way that the Manhattan Project decision was inefficient. However, the identical consequences attended. There is no more reliable means of achieving scientific progress than promoting widespread interest in any given problem and thereby maximizing the opportunity for participation. Pluralism is, therefore, the guiding hand behind scientific progress. The quite incredible scientific and technological advances achieved in the past few hundred years would not have been possible if an "efficient" system of problem allocation had been in place. Without pluralism, stagnation – not ebullient progress – would have been the inevitable consequence.

* * *

"Whereas, in order to the finding out of the longitude of places for perfecting navigation and astronomy,

we have resolved to build a small observatory within Our Park at Greenwich."

With this proclamation, Charles II of England highlighted the importance to Britain as an emerging sea power, of the proper measurement of longitude to facilitate navigation of the world's oceans. King Charles founded the Royal Observatory in 1675 to solve the problem of establishing longitude at sea.

It was at that time understood that for every 15° traveled eastward, the local time moved one hour ahead. Similarly, in traveling westward 15°, local time moved back one hour. Knowing the local times at two points on Earth, allows for the determination of the longitudinal difference between them. This idea was very important to sailors and navigators in the 17th century. By observing the sun, they could identify local noontime anywhere. Navigation required that they also know the time at some reference point (e.g. Greenwich) in order to calculate their longitude. No clock existing in the 17th century could maintain accuracy when exposed to the motions of a ship at sea and the changes encountered in temperature and humidity.

The Royal Observatory at this time developed a set of tables for determining the moon's position relative to bright stars as a means to calculate the time at Greenwich. Sailors could measure the moon's position relative to these stars and use the tables to calculate Greenwich time in comparison with their own local time. This means of finding longitude was known as the "Lunar Distance Method." However, the extreme difficulty of achieving accurate sightings even when the moon was visible in the night sky made the determination of longitude by this technique extremely uncertain. It became clear that a clock that could faithfully and accurately maintain Greenwich time, was an essential maritime need.

In 1714, the British Government offered, by Act of Parliament,

> "a prize of £20,000 for any solution which could provide longitude to within half-a-degree (2 minutes of time). The methods would be tested on a ship, sailing . . . over the ocean, from Great Britain to any such Port in the West Indies as those Commissioners Choose . . . without losing their Longitude beyond the limits before mentioned and should prove to be . . . tried and found Practicable and Useful at Sea."

A Board of Longitude was set up to administer and judge applications for the longitude prize. They received many weird and wonderful suggestions. Many people believed that the problem simply could not be solved. However, an open-ended offer of this magnitude had the inestimable benefit of tapping into the concept of pluralism. No one knew where a solution might come from, but anyone with an idea could engage in the search. The pot of gold at the end of this rainbow offered a substantial incentive.

The rest of the story by which John Harrison, a working class joiner (carpenter) from Lincolnshire, with little formal education, took on the scientific and academic establishment of his time and finally won the longitude prize in 1773 through extraordinary mechanical insight, talent and determination is well known.

On his second voyage of discovery, Captain James Cook carried with him Harrison's chronometer. He returned in July 1775, after a voyage of three years, which ranged from the tropics to Antarctica. Longitudinal measurements showed the daily rate of Harrison's chronometer never to vary by more than 8 seconds (corresponding to a distance of 2 nautical miles at the equator) during the entire voyage.

Cook referred to the watch as "... our faithful guide through all the vicissitudes of climates."

* * *

Many other examples of pluralism, promoted by the awarding of prizes for solutions to problems, can be cited. For instance, the French Academy in 1775 offered a prize of 12,000 francs for anyone who could develop artificial alkali. Nicolas Leblanc won this prize based on his observations of the reaction between sulfuric acid and common salt. This work led to the growth of the 19th century inorganic chemical industry.

One of the many prizes important to the practical development of the aeronautical industry, the Orteig prize of $25,000 for the pilot who would fly solo, non-stop from New York to Paris, was famously won in 1927 by Charles Lindbergh.

More recently in 1959, the Kremer prize of £50,000 for developing a human powered aircraft that could fly a one-mile, figure eight course was established. The American, Paul MacCready, won it some 18 years later.

Finally, a few years ago, SpaceShipOne developed by Burt

Rutan and his American team of engineers – one of twenty-seven competing teams from seven countries – won the $10 million X prize, by achieving sub-orbital flight for three people and then repeating the accomplishment within two weeks. Private sector participation in space exploration has followed.

* * *

The unexpected collapse of the Soviet Union in 1991 focused attention on its failure to achieve anything like the economic performance of not only the industrialized nations of the West, but even those of such third world countries as Korea and Taiwan. The root cause of this failure was obscured by the cold war's ideological confrontations – the communist system vs. western democracy. In reality, however, it was simply a lack of economic pluralism that was largely responsible for the sorry plight of the Soviet economy.

In modern times, the rate of growth in the wealth of nations has been found to correlate overwhelmingly with the extent to which individuals in those nations have the ease and freedom to pursue economic activities. Generally, the more centralized is economic decision-making, the lower is the rate of growth that can be expected, whether the nation has been democratic, like India, or autocratic, like China. We are currently seeing in both these nations, an accelerated rate of economic growth consequent upon the deliberate freeing up of economic decision-making.

An earlier example of this inexorable correlation is to be found in a comparison of the economic development of two small island nations, Taiwan and Cuba, after both succumbed to postwar dictatorships. In Taiwan where political suppression was unaccompanied by economic centralization, economic development proceeded apace and Taiwan was already a wealthy nation when democratic reform commenced. Cuba, where political suppression and centralized economic planning continue to this day, is a poor and stagnant nation.

The logic of economic pluralism is the foundation of western market economics and Adam Smith's invisible hand. When millions of potential decision-makers are the resource for a solution to a potential customer desire, that desire will be perceived and solutions will quickly and reliably follow. The centralization of this decision-making function creates the need for god-like prescience in order to achieve comparable performance. Such economies have amply demonstrated the enormity of human fallibility. Pluralism is an essential feature present in the economy of prosperous nations.

* * *

That pluralism is a concept so fundamental to the dynamic progress of science and technology, and the dynamic growth of Western economies, suggests some obvious questions.

Why is there little evidence today that this concept of pluralism is integral to the problem solving efforts employed to address the societal ills highlighted in the prologue?

Why do governments not seek to offer the incentives to help create the motivational environment that will promote such problem solving, as a challenge to be widely engaged by many sectors of our societies? Why do they instead see themselves as capable of legislating solutions?

If the concept of pluralism were widely appreciated and applied, a much different form of legislation could emerge from government deliberations. These would contribute to the better outcomes needed if we are to escape from our current troubled evolutionary path.

Chapter III

*S*cale

Our economy has come to be defined by large businesses. A financial system uniquely suited to encourage and support their growth and profitability has become a dominant feature of this economy. Recent events (2008-2013) have shown a darker side to this apparently successful business model. This has implications germane to the future evolution of our economy.

I began my own business career in 1964 in Montreal with the founding of Pulmac Research Ltd. The name Pulmac had its origin as a holding company (Pulmac Ltd.) that my father set up to receive and distribute royalties from the sale of equipment that he had designed, patented and licensed for manufacture. The name is a contraction of "pulp machinery", the area in which his inventive ideas were focused. This also applied to a principal area of my own research activity.

My business offered research and development services to non-competing firms in the pulp, paper and allied industries. These were offered on an on-going basis using my own laboratory facilities, on a scale appropriate to each client's operational and financing capabilities. Relationships were developed with a number of paper industry equipment suppliers. The experiences of my early years further demonstrated that applying the scientific approach, so successful in my Scottish years, readily developed novel and scientifically sound ideas for client businesses. These pointed the way for significant improvements in the performance or operational efficiency of their equipment.

My initial lack of experience in sales and marketing contributed to difficulties encountered in promoting this business model. Additionally, I found that smaller companies using my services, while having no problem moving from research ideas to development and marketing phases, frequently ran into financial difficulties. This delayed or terminated projects.

Larger businesses, on the other hand, seemed to have all sorts of bureaucratic obstacles preventing a smooth transition from a successful research phase to the more expensive development effort needed to establish marketable products.

In one area of client research having to do with pulp drainage, I borrowed old laboratory equipment that had been used in pioneering research work at McGill University in Montreal. This equipment produced extremely useful data. The apparatus itself, however, was cumbersome and time-consuming in its measuring procedures. However, it became clear that an instrument with the ability to generate such data easily and rapidly should prove of general interest to pulp and paper research laboratories around the world. This led to a decision to develop such an instrument – the Pulmac Permeability tester. This exercise proved quite successful, resulting in a dozen or so quick sales. This produced cash flow based on initial investment, rather than cash flow based on current effort – as did client research work.

The difficulty I encountered in building up the client base for my research activity, together with the retention problems I encountered due to small client cash flow problems or larger client unwillingness to move beyond a modest research effort, made the experience of generating income by selling an instrument very attractive indeed. Therefore, I began moving away from my original business model by investing as much time as possible researching ideas for product development that I could exploit myself.

This shift in emphasis ultimately initiated activity in three areas. The successful outcome of building and selling a new instrument created the incentive to develop additional instruments. This led to the founding of Pulmac Instruments Ltd., to conduct and promote that activity. Over the next several years this effort yielded two new and novel instruments – the Pulmac Shive Analyzer and the Pulmac Zero Span Tester. This resulted in a new focus on market development in this area.

In this same time frame I revisited extensive research work

I had undertaken for two past clients. One had terminated because of severe financial problems, the other when purchased by a much larger company. These data were sufficiently advanced that I was able to conceive of novel designs for new process equipment with patentable features. With the help of an engineering partner, I founded two new development companies that ultimately contracted with different large machinery supply companies to further develop and then market these inventions under fee and royalty agreements.

Finally I became involved entrepreneurially with two other partners in the development of a small business computer accounting package for use on time-share computers. In the late 1960s this was the only affordable means by which small businesses could access computer power. My role in this new business, working with a brilliant software programmer and an experienced office product salesman, was to identify the small business accounting needs to be incorporated into the accounting package. Further, I tested out the resulting software by using it to handle all the accounting functions and financial analyses for my other businesses.

By the mid 1970s the instrument business was progressing well, the development businesses were bringing in increasing royalty income and the computer business had gotten off the ground with a venture capital assist. However, life in Montreal had become complicated. A secessionist party, the Partie Québécois, came to power in Quebec in 1976. Its goal to separate Quebec from Canada became a focus for Quebec nationalism. I felt that this aberration would take at least a generation to subside and in the meantime produce a political environment devoid of much meaning for me. In addition, the instrument business had become intimately connected into the U.S. economy. It supplied the bulk of the standard components incorporated into the instruments we built and was the major destination for their sales. The duty and brokerage costs of the resulting two-way flow of Pulmac goods across the U.S.-Canadian border had become significant. The decision to emigrate and move the business to Vermont logically followed.

By the time I moved in 1978, I had sold out my interest in the computer company and concentrated my attention on building up cash flow in the instrument business and on the research work needed to continue the development of new instruments. The royalty income from the development businesses made it possible for me to invest significant time doing such research. I also limited my sales and marketing activities in the instrument business to a level sufficient only to ensure sales adequate to cover operating costs. This made available further time for research, an activity now vital to my plans for developing future revenues.

I purchased an old farm property with a farmhouse and barn on 5 acres of land near Montpelier. The barn exterior camouflaged the interior construction of a modern building to provide space for the administrative, assembly and laboratory operations for the instrument business. And so I settled into a new life in Vermont.

I have given this overview of my business experiences so

that an important aspect of my life in Vermont will be comprehensible. Leaving the Montreal suburb where I had lived for some fifteen years ended a variety of community activities. Upon arriving in Vermont, this left a void in my life. Happenstance brought me into the sphere of what in Vermont is termed "small" business. I became involved with a local economic development group that sought to increase economic activity by promoting business education for the local small business community. I volunteered my time and ended up leading this activity. Thus began an extended period in which I explored the meaning of "small" business and the nature of beneficial small business education against the backdrop of my own business experiences.

Although my business activities typically employed less than a dozen people, I previously would not have characterized myself as anything but a businessman. Now, in Vermont, I was being categorized as a "small" businessman.

This led me to investigate what special meaning should be associated with this terminology. For twenty-five years following my arrival in Vermont I spent time exploring this question. I helped to establish the Vermont Small Business Network (SBN), through which I was involved over the years in hundreds of business discussions with many local small business owners. I edited and published a bimonthly newsletter for the SBN. I helped organize and participated in annual SBN small business conferences. I developed course material and periodically over this period taught small business education courses as a means to test out evolving ideas. I read widely in the business literature to support these activities. The ideas important to the theme of this chapter evolved during this period of my life.

I recognized that the manner in which I conducted my business activities was quite different from the more structured approach of my large company clients and customers. Initially I considered this simply a consequence of personal idiosyncrasy. However, in talking with other Vermont small business owners, I discovered a broad commonality in our attitudes and approaches to our business activities. SBN discussion groups fostered honest interactions that identified uncertainties and failures as well as things that seemed to work well. These discussions suggested we were operating our businesses in a different "space" from that occupied by the classic American corporation. However, this space was not unique to each of us, but common to all of us. I came to think of this as "the small business space" and began to explore and study its contours and characteristics.

I was particularly interested in how these differed from the normal business space described in text books, taught in business schools, analyzed in the *Harvard Business Review* and described in such business publications as *The Wall Street Journal* and *Forbes Magazine.*

People who operate small businesses are typically their owners. This gives them operational opportunities inconceivable in large organizations. Much that is taught in business schools and presented in the textbooks they employ – while clearly relevant and useful for those planning to work in major corporations – is frequently misleading or inapplicable in the small business context. My thinking and analyses in this area led me to modify and enhance many practices in my own business as my understanding of the unique aspects of the small business space evolved.

I identified basic practices that clearly distinguished operations in the small business space from conventional business practices. I led discussion groups focused on these ideas, receiving much positive feedback from many local small business owners. They all recognized they readily fit into the framework I was building.

One fundamental distinction between large and small businesses has to do with "motivation." In public corporations (also known as publicly owned or publicly traded corporations) the personal motives of management must necessarily be subordinated to the profit and growth imperative demanded by shareholders and financial markets. This creates a potential source of on-going tension.

Consider a CEO of a public corporation personally motivated to create a product of "great benefit to humanity" but clearly a less likely money-maker than alternative investment opportunities. Under such circumstances the executive would be unlikely even to try and convince a board of directors to allow him or her to follow this dream.

By contrast, the motivation that drives a small business is necessarily that of its owners. A small business has the freedom to establish as a primary motive the development of excellence in the achievement of personal goals. Although the cash flows necessary to sustain the business are an important concern, they can be conceived as a natural by-product of achieving excellence in meeting customer needs or wants. Thus while "making money" is necessary, in no sense need it be the primary business motive. Growth may or may not be requisite to the achievement of such business goals but certainly need have no meaning as a stand-alone motive.

Most small business people I have met operate their businesses, as did I, very much aware of the need to generate the necessary cash flows, but confident that such would be the outcome once goals framed in very different terms than "making money," were met.

This means that the purpose and goals of any small business can be given broad appeal. A uniform motivation can thus embrace owners and employees alike. This is impossible to sustain in a large public corporation.

This leads to a second fundamental distinction between large and small businesses. This concerns employee productivity – the "actual" in relation to the "potential" contribution of each employee to the success of the business.

To avoid chaos, large businesses require hierarchical structures to manage the activities of their many employees. This necessarily places constraints on employee activities. Employees are expected to fit a job description and function reliably within its constraints. Such constraints act to discourage employees from giving efforts beyond a normal level acceptable to management.

In small businesses employees can be treated as individuals capable of gaining understanding of the detailed functions of the business. They can then be given the opportunity and encouraged to optimize their role in the business, in a sense, more as partners than employees. The possibilities opened up by this kind of freedom, together with the motivational environment to pursue such possibilities, are not to be found in large corporations. This offers to small businesses the possibility for achieving far higher levels of individual employee productivity than can possibly be sustained in any large business.

These fundamental distinctions allow for significant operational differences. Small businesses have the opportunity to become far more people-oriented. This applies not only to employees, but also to customers and suppliers. Appreciating that these interconnected relationships work best for a business when serious attention is given to how they can be made "mutually" beneficial produces important results.

By way of example, in my instrument business we carefully developed as close relationships as possible with vendor sales people. We encouraged them to visit our rural location at any time without appointment, to suit their schedule, with a cup of coffee and someone in the organization always available. We stressed the importance to us of reliable service and delivery as well as price, and were loyal customers of those who met these needs.

This attention resulted in these sales people wanting to help us; e.g. identifying alternative components, even ones they couldn't themselves supply. They helped ensure overnight emergency deliveries to us the odd times that circumstances required such efforts. In effect, we became important to these individuals in a personal way that went beyond normal commercial services. They actually cared and wanted to be a part of our success.

To enhance this relationship we published a company newsletter speaking to both the professional and social aspects of our business, with profiles of employees as well as contact people from supplier companies. This was mailed to all of our suppliers, professional people whose services we engaged as well as to certain customers.

Large businesses require procedures to be put in place that create a more formal environment. For instance in my dealings with them I found it virtually impossible to make a successful cold call – a sales meeting without an appointment. Even making such appointments didn't prevent my frequently having to wait for extended periods before connecting with the actual customer. These realities are obviously not conducive to establishing anything beyond a strictly commercial relationship.

My business focused the attention of our employees on understanding the basic functions and aspirations of the business. We stressed that their paychecks although distributed by us came from our customers. We insisted they keep this foremost in their minds every time they received a customer call. We discussed ways in which we might support employee lifestyle interests as part of employment benefits: e.g. providing flexible work hours to accommodate some specific outside activities on an on-going basis.

We stressed that their value to the company was determined by the quality and reliability of their performance, and the extent to which such services could be rendered with minimum demands on our management time. We also encouraged them to think how better to perform aspects of their routine work and to propose ways of "growing" their job responsibilities. We stressed that we only employed people who were "essential" to our business success, and therefore wanted them to execute a necessary role as part of a well-coordinated team effort.

The size of their labor force, even when not unionized, prevents large companies from individualizing employee work relationships in the manner discussed above.

In my business we considered customer relationships as a search for customer "sanction". We were introducing new ideas and equipment into a conservative industry and sought creative approaches to encourage accessible employees in prospective pulp or paper mills to view themselves as participants in helping meet this challenge. We sought to maintain close and supportive post-sales relationships with these people. We wanted them to feel they were part of the successful spread of new ideas within the industry and to support our efforts, thereby sanctioning our activities.

These few examples of others I could cite represent feasible strategies that can be successfully pursued only because the necessary attitudes and authority to enhance the development of such relationships can be spread to everyone in the organization. In the small business space this is feasible. My experiences with large corporations made it obvious that they could only pay lip service to any such strategies. Most employees in such organizations lack the authority and therefore the incentive to function in the ways I have described.

Over this extended period I interacted daily with the corporate world that was my instrument company's customer base. At the same time I was thinking about the nature and opportunities open to me through the pursuit and testing of ideas applicable only in the newly conceived small business space.

I began to consider the possibility that corporate America, as the driving force of our economy, was perhaps an historical anomaly. Could it be that the life and times of large corporate entities are presently at an apogee, but fated to wane, as did the dominance of those other dinosaurs some 65 million years ago?

In *The Origin of Species* Charles Darwin presented nature's evidence that all life on this planet is the consequence of an inexorable process of random organic change, introducing new characteristics to a species, some of which prove beneficial when interacting with an often-hostile environment. The result is an increasingly diverse and complex array of life forms, each mastering its survival in a particular environmental niche.

It is plausible that this process ultimately produced sapient humanity from single-celled progenitors. It is equally plausible that human societal evolution as deduced from the historical record is analogous to organic evolution, even if a more conscious process.

The evolution of our species is no longer determined primarily by the random mutation of genes, but rather by the conscious efforts of humanity to beneficially alter societal organization. In this sense the outcomes in societal evolution are similar to those achieved by organic evolution. What most benefits societal success drives the process of societal evolution just as what most benefited species survival drove the process of organic evolution.

Darwin thus introduced the essential character of evolution as a general process driven by forces ultimately beyond the control of individuals. The acts of individuals can promote or impede humanity's societal evolution. Inexorably, however, humanity will, in the long run, advance its societal organization and related structures in whatever direction is most beneficial to its people even though that direction, at any given time, may be difficult if not impossible to discern.

Three hundred years ago the entire population of Europe was under 100 million. Overwhelmingly it consisted of tenant farmers, crafts people, and workers attracted to the factories of the early industrial revolution. Poverty was the normal condition of most of the population.

These Europeans were the ancestral source for much of the current U.S. population of some 300 million people. Many of these now own houses and cars and enjoy a standard of living that would have been inconceivable to their ancestors of 300 years ago.

The clearest distinction that can be drawn between 18th century Europe and 21st century America is the huge increase in society's ability to generate wealth. Since wealth creation has generally been beneficial to society it is not unreasonable to suggest that increasing wealth creation is a de facto beneficial force in societal evolution.

Economists summarize wealth formation with a measurable statistic familiar to all as the GNP, the gross national product. This is simply the summation of economic exchanges annually recorded in the statistics of a nation's economic activity. It follows that wealth generation is manifest in the rate of exchange of goods and services. The greater and more productive is this rate, the greater will be the wealth generated.

Over the past 300 years the source of exchangeable goods and services has largely shifted from individuals acting alone or with apprentices, or in small groups, to increasingly larger groups of individuals organized in "businesses". These businesses are now the essential vehicles for wealth creation and thus for the betterment of our societies.

Nevertheless business is frequently considered as a necessary evil. Profit is often considered tainted if not immoral. Much of this attitude has roots in the historical process by which industrial development and employee exploitation went hand-in-hand.

It is time to recognize the fact that businesses have developed, through societal evolution, as an important means for social progress. What has lagged behind is consideration of how the business entity itself should evolve so that it will most effectively fulfill its role in support of our evolutionary progress.

The growth to dominance of the large public corporation is a product of the late 19th and early 20th centuries. Mass production was the only viable means to reduce unit costs to the low level required in order to sell the burgeoning variety of consumer goods that rampant technological advances of that time made possible. The large organizations and the large investments required to finance the capability to mass-produce and then to market and distribute its products inevitably led to large public corporations financed through the sale of common shares to the general public.

The trend to larger and larger corporate entities has been a dominant feature since the last quarter of the 20th century. The million dollar corporate mergers of the 1960s and 70s have become the billion dollar merges of today. The question that seems never to be seriously posed is whether this trend has any societal benefit.

Logically, the only social justification for increasing the size of any business is that its ability to innovate with new products or to improve the quality of existing products or to reduce the price of its products requires such an increase. Only in that way can it be argued that a net societal benefit will attend corporate growth. For many large corporate entities existing today, it is very doubtful that their growth has been attended by any of the above-suggested societal benefits.

In my professional lifetime, I have witnessed dramatic consolidation producing much larger corporate entities of the companies that produce pulp and paper and those that provide goods and services to that industry. I have not observed any corresponding societal benefits as described above – in fact, quite the opposite.

The paper industry has become notably less internally innovative over the years. When I first entered the industry an upward trend in the employment of scientists like myself was evident. Over time this reversed and mills came to rely almost entirely on suppliers for any productivity or quality improvements.

A demand that specific benefits be guaranteed meant paying the higher prices such a policy required. Also senior management became increasingly divorced from the operating floor.

Management in the paper industry is now increasingly driven by the dictates of short-term financial performance and wholly focused on using size to gain control of market supply and thereby enhancing control of pricing. All this has been at the expense of any real efforts at quality or efficiency improvements internally at the operational level.

The excoriation of upper management by mill technical and production people in conversations I had during mill visits had become, over time, increasingly common. It is unlikely that my observations of the consequences of consolidation in the paper industry are unique to that industry. The general applicability of these observations seems more likely.

Why, then, have we so overwhelmingly engaged in a practice that is so questionable from the perspective of the overarching needs for effective societal evolution?

I believe the answer to this question is that the concept of "economies of size", so relevant a factor in the growth and consolidation of the industrial revolution has become a de facto dogma – an a priori presumption beyond questioning.

The diseconomies of growth associated with necessary additional organizational overheads, with inevitable degradation of individual labor productivity, with increasingly difficult communication, control and response functions, with reduced flexibility and more political diversions of energy, etc., are typically ignored.

The enormous technical changes I have experienced over the course of my professional career, have transformed the capability, capacity and productivity options available to small business owners.

Through my entrepreneurial activities, the advent of the time-share computer allowed me, for the first time, to integrate and effectively utilize budgeting and timely financial reporting to support my business planning and execution. The development of the personal computer made these and many other software services widely available and affordable to small businesses. I came to use computers in every aspect of my business. They became vital tools for myself, and everyone I employed.

The arrival of FedEx and UPS, of the fax machine and then of e-mail and the Internet, made it possible to support global sales of my equipment in a way that had previously been impossible. Continuing technical advances in the Internet greatly enhance opportunities for more effective, more economical, and more geographically expansive marketing and sales support than ever before. Advances in computer control of machine tools allowed the small machine shops my business dealt with, to greatly reduce their manufacturing costs on our behalf. Developments in robotics promise to make new and even more spectacular future automation options affordable to small businesses.

The essential point to appreciate is that these technical developments have transformed the capability of small business operations. These improvements increasingly include efficiencies previously available only through economies of size. I have fully experienced this sea change that has greatly diminished the advantages large companies have traditionally gained through economies of size.

What meaning should be taken from this?

We are stuck in a time warp. We believe that "large" organizations are the means that best deliver economic and societal benefits as the cited evidence to the contrary mounts. The impact of new technology is constantly eroding the previous logic that dictated the emergence of large organizations. The time has come to reassess this logic. This applies equally to all large organizations, whether corporations, non-profits, or government agencies.

We need to give thought to the proposition that the most productive organizations to deal with any of society's needs or wants, private sector or public sector, will necessarily be the smallest rather than the largest that can be conceived to accomplish the particular mission.

This is contrary to current practice. Nevertheless, the effective problem solving needed to redirect our societies' evolutionary paths will, I believe, be advanced more successfully once this important concept of "optimum scale" is properly understood and acted upon.

Outcomes

Chapter IV

The Economy

Nowhere in the area of human studies does scientific thinking seem more obviously absent than in the field of economics. The response to the 2008 economic collapse provides a dramatic illustration.

Although the remedial actions that have been proposed by the economics profession have varied in emphasis and detail, they have all been based on the same assumption: The existing economic system needs only an improved regulatory framework, if of a disputed nature, and appropriate government policies, again much disputed, to reestablish the same functioning economy that has benefited us in the past.

That the functioning of the economic system itself might be structurally flawed, requiring fundamental changes rather than simply seeking to re-establish the status quo, has nowhere been suggested.

The scientific attribute of "disbelieving" and therefore questioning existing basic practices can nowhere be found in mainstream economic writings or reporting.

Our evolutionary journey, as emphasized in the prologue, informs that our survival and wellbeing are now a consequence of how well we structure and organize our societies. This means creating an environment that seeks to maximize the productive output of our citizenry in contributing to the production and distribution of the goods and services now responsible for our survival and wellbeing.

The current economic system functions in such a way as to repeatedly place formidable barriers preventing citizens from best contributing to this overall wellbeing because of involuntary unemployment. This is a recurring feature of the modern economy, considered normal by the economics profession, to be ameliorated by the proper, if much disputed, role of government.

Since an economic system is a human contrivance that is not constrained by any inviolable physical laws, recurring failures should suggest the possibility of flaws in current economic thinking. Structural defects might exist that need to be identified and reformed. Unfortunately, the economics' profession lacks the scientific discipline to challenge long held, but now highly questionable, beliefs.

We need to look elsewhere for inspiration.

Bill Krehm is an unusual man. I have known him all my life as an uncle by marriage. I came to appreciate him in this new way only after reconnecting upon my return to Canada from my sojourn in Scotland and after I had commenced my career as a research and development specialist.

Bill was a Marxist soapbox speaker in his youth, growing up in Toronto during the depression years of the 1930s. He has since pursued a broad range of interests that account for his being unusual. He speaks several languages fluently, and has a reading knowledge of several more. He is not only an accomplished violinist himself but for some years was music critic for a major daily newspaper in Toronto. He studied journalism and was at one time a foreign correspondent for Time magazine. He has also been a freelance literary critic.

These aspects of his life ended in the mid 1950s when a review of his income in relation to his perceived needs to finance the future education of two young sons set him on a new course. He borrowed and invested to purchase and build apartment buildings and became a landlord and developer. The exceptional immigrant population growth in Toronto at this time helped this investment to quickly pay off. By the early 1960s he was prospering in his new trade.

At this time a new 11% tax on all building materials was levied by the central government. Having studied mathematics at the University of Chicago, Bill was well equipped to make a careful analysis of the impact that this new tax would have on his development business.

He acted upon his conclusions by selling all his apartment buildings and investing the proceeds in the purchase of old mansion-style houses in downtown areas of Toronto. The flight to the suburbs and property tax increases in the core city had made these properties unattractive and unwanted. Bill had no trouble cornering the market in such housing. These he subdivided into highly marketable apartments.

His analysis had convinced him that an 11% increase in the cost of building materials would translate into a major increase in the cost to build new apartment buildings, forcing the price of rentals upward and squeezing profit margins. The cost to add to the stock of rental apartments by renovating large old houses purchased at market depressed prices would be far lower and therefore far more profitable than constructing new apartment buildings.

Events proved Bill correct and by the mid 60s he had several million dollars to show for it. But as I said, Bill is an unusual man. His response to his success was to stabilize his business to give himself a profitable return as a landlord, and allow him time to focus his attention on economic theory.

Now why on earth should he do that? Well, Bill recognized that his analysis correctly predicted that a tax levied by the central government would appear as an increase in the price for new rental apartments. He was also sufficiently well read to appreciate that macroeconomic theory denied this possibility. So he wanted to find out where economic theory had gone wrong. His approach was simple. He began with Adam Smith and commenced to read every subsequent book of any significance to the field of economic study in whatever language it had been originally published. This took him several years by which time he had developed clear ideas of how and where economic theory had gone wrong. It was about this time that I became a sounding board for these ideas, beginning my own slow progress toward economic literacy.

I had taken a course in macroeconomics somewhere in my academic past, but could only recall that it never made much sense to me. Now I had a new incentive – trying to get my mind around Bill's new ideas. The more I delved into these matters the greater became my conviction that my earliest assessment of macroeconomic theory was in fact prescient. It didn't make any sense to me because indeed it was nonsensical.

The French economist Léon Walras (1834-1910) is widely regarded as the father of general equilibrium theory, which he first elucidated in his 1874 publication, *Elements of Pure Economics*. His general equilibrium theory applied the concepts of calculus to define the price of any goods or services offered in the market place. Accordingly, this price is determined as the point at which the supply and demand curves for such goods or services intersect. If supply increases faster than demand, the intersection of the supply-demand curves slides backwards to a lower price. Conversely if demand exceeds supply this intersection point slides forward to a higher price.

Anyone familiar with economics 101 will recognize this, since the self-balancing, general equilibrium theory is still taught as fundamental to modern economic thought. It is also the reigning dogma followed by the Federal Reserve Board as it seeks to nudge supply or demand curves in the direction of price stability, thereby fighting inflation by perceived appropriate interest rate adjustments.

Bill's entry point into economic theory was the very tangible reality that a government tax increase had increased prices in his field of activity. His actions based on the prediction that this would happen, earned him several million dollars – evidence not to be sneezed at! Why had this occurred if prices were, in fact, solely determined by the interaction of supply with demand? Bill recognized that these *"irreducible and stubborn facts"* meant that equilibrium theory as presently understood could not be sustained.

It must be wrong.

By the early 1970s Bill's economic odyssey had led him to appreciate that many societal developments of the mid 20th century were entering the economic sphere as independent contributors to general price increases. These included the burgeoning role of government, the cost impact of new safety, employment and environmental regulations, insurance costs associated with increasing liability litigation, and other such non-market forces. Equilibrium theory needed to be repositioned to account for these new factors that gave to prices a new component independent of supply or demand.

This component, in fact, was now playing a role in the determination of the supply-demand relationship itself, rather than the other way around. In discussions at that time, Bill pointed out that in the United States, the combined effect of many of these forces including the Johnson-era funding of both the Vietnam war and his domestic war on poverty, would, in due course, produce a pronounced and general increase in prices. Such increases, misinterpreted as supply-demand inflation, would cause the Federal Reserve Board to increase interest rates bringing on a recession with increasing unemployment.

However, in defiance of equilibrium theory, although unemployment figures would increase, prices would also continue to rise. This simultaneous increase in unemployment and the general level of prices being contrary to current equilibrium theory would, according to Bill, awaken professional economists to the need for fresh thinking.

Bill's prediction about the American economy showed up in the Carter years with then Chairman of the Federal Reserve Board, Paul Voelker, pushing interest rates upward into the double digits and producing a severe recession. This was not initially attended by any moderation in price increases. Only after a substantial period of time, did the much lauded stabilization of prices occur.

The other side of Bill's prediction, however, that economists would heed the simultaneous increase in unemployment with rising prices, as a call for new thinking, proved erroneous. The response was simply to label the phenomenon as "stagflation" in the belief that this somehow saved the situation.

As a scientist I fully appreciated that a conjecture when formulated as a risky prediction is particularly persuasive when it proves correct. So, when Bill's prediction about the American economy proved correct, it made a deep impression. I began to read more widely in the field. This included the ideas that Bill Krehm and others of his ilk have published over the past 40 years. Bill himself has published a number of books[1], three of which deal with his critique of general equilibrium theory as it is currently espoused.

1. *Price in a Mixed Economy, Our Record of Disaster (1975)*
   Babel's Tower, The Dynamics of Economic Breakdown (1977)
   How to Make Money in a Mismanaged Economy (1980);

Thornwood Publications, 141 Avenue Road, Toronto, Ontario, M5R 2H7.

These include his ideas for repositioning that theory to bring it into accord with the workings of the actual economy. He also has illuminated the sorry consequences resulting from the failure to do so.

Bill was also instrumental in setting up the Toronto-based COMER, the *Committee on Monetary and Economic Reform*, as a center for contrarian economic analysis and discussion. Only a year or so ago at the age of one hundred, did Bill retire as editor and major contributor to the increasingly influential *Economic Reform*, COMER's official newsletter. (http://www.comer.org). But, as I have already said, Bill is an unusual man.

My connection with COMER led me to meet a number of its leading figures. One of these was another non-academic, economic scholar by the name of Bill Hixson. His background was amazingly similar to that of Bill Krehm. He also was a depression era Marxist, then subsequently a successful engineer and businessman whose business experiences also led him to question current economic theory. My association with Hixson focused my attention on the second great anomaly of our economic system.

The concept of money evolved as a natural part of the evolution of civilizations. The earliest coins that have been discovered were minted in Lydia about 640 BC from an amalgam of gold and silver. This use of gold and silver coinage as money gradually became widespread. Gold became a major source of societal wealth as well as the medium of exchange that supported the increasingly mercantile activities of Europe's middle ages.

War and pillage became important means by which the wealth of nations and their ability to support the expansion of their trade and commerce could be sustained. The sack of Constantinople in 1204 during the fourth crusade and the 16th century pillage of the Aztec and Inca civilizations by the Spanish conquistadors resulted in very significant injections of gold into the economies of Europe. These were crucial for their economic development over these periods.

Banks have been around for almost as long as money. Initially they were solely repositories to safeguard surplus valuables, the ancient equivalent of modern day strong boxes and vaults. At some point receipts given to owners of stored valuables came to be used as proof of credibility and then as credit worthiness. Once the minting of coins became widespread, banking practices expanded into the business of usury, or the lending out of monies for repayment with interest.

The receipt morphed into the bank promissory note, entitling the bearer to an exchange for some denomination of gold. As people became used to these bank notes and comfortable with them as redeemable proxies for gold, these notes began to exchange for goods and services without the bother of preliminary conversion to coin. When customers began accepting promissory notes from banks for purposes of exchange, it was easier for them to simply leave their gold safely in banks.

Bankers then realized that they could readily issue more bank notes than could be redeemed by their gold stock, since redemption of coin was generally quickly offset by redeposit of coin. Bankers could then lend out the same money to multiple borrowers, greatly increasing profits. The temptation to print ever-increasing quantities of notes on a fixed store of gold was frequently irresistible. If rumors of such practices began to circulate, more and more people would be inclined to redeem their gold, ultimately producing a "run" on the bank, potentially causing its failure (bankruptcy) with many depositors being left out in the cold.

What was clearly in the bankers' best interests frequently also served the economic interests of the communities in which they operated. When local economies sought to expand while gold coin was locally in short supply, the "new" money created by excessive bank note production made the economic expansion possible.

This private banking system was the driving force for economic expansion in the western world from the beginnings of the industrial revolution until the great depression of the 1930s. Only a modest but increasing involvement of national governments in regularizing the minting and distribution of coinage occurred in this time. This whole period was also characterized by intervals of severe dislocation when conditions prompted the psychological concerns that led to bank runs, bank failures, and economic contractions.

The Great Depression of the 1930s marked a turning point. Its severity forced national governments to intervene. Public regulation of the banking system was introduced and the authority of central banking was greatly strengthened. Confidence in the credit worthiness of the nation state replaced that of individual banks. However, the basic mechanisms for money creation, though now regulated, remained essentially unchanged as a stable feature of the private sector of the economy.

This simplified historical perspective reinforces an important point: the monetary system that now dominates our world has been determined by historical forces and is commonly accepted, uncritically, simply as the way things are.

The modern, so-called, fractional reserve system has simply institutionalized the old time banker's judgment as to the quantity of promissory notes that can be safely issued, over and above the amount of actual gold held in their vaults. To keep it simple, if today a billion dollars was invested in a bank start-up, the bank would then be authorized by the federal government, in accordance with the fractional reserve system, to make consumer and business loans (thereby increasing their deposits) totaling somewhat more than 10 billion dollars. The 1 billion of cash represents the "reserves" which become the "fraction" of the loans (deposits) that the fractional reserve system authorizes.

This leveraged amount of money is created by such bank loans, out of thin air so-to-speak, entering the bank accounts of the borrowers and then circulating as "new" money into the economy.

When the Federal Reserve decides that the economy would benefit from more new money, as has been the case recently, it typically purchases government securities thus injecting new money into the financial system. This new money increases the reserves of the banking system, allowing them to themselves (according to the fractional reserve system) create some ten times more new money by increasing their loan portfolios.

Bill Hixson can now enter the picture with his penetrating analysis of a monetary system so taken for granted that not even professional economists, let alone the general public, give it much thought. By the latter, it is generally considered too complex a matter to be understood, so that even a rudimentary appreciation of money creation through the fractional reserve system, fundamental to private banking, is frequently lacking. For the professionals, individual aspects of the monetary system seem to be understood but poorly integrated in their consciousness and never a focus for critical thought.

Hixson remedies these deficiencies in his book, *A Matter of Interest* [2]. His refreshing approach is based on an intensive analysis of actual statistical data. These are to be found in *The National Income and Product Accounts* of the Bureau

of Economic Analysis and the *Flow of Funds Accounts* of the
Federal Reserve System.

*2. A Matter of Interest. Reexamining Money,
    Debt, and Real Economic Growth.*
Praeger Publishers, One Madison Avenue, New York, NY 10010 (1991)

While far from perfect, these data are consistent over time
and allow for a coherent analysis of the big economic picture,
which Hixson proceeds to do. The following are key points
from Hixson's extensive and detailed analysis of the U.S.
economy from 1918 to 1987 which I find particularly impressive, and persuasive of his basic conclusions.

Hixson supplies data comparing economic growth (GNP)
and the increase in the money supply at different periods over
a hundred year span beginning in 1880. These data inform
that growth of economic activity is always accompanied by a
corresponding growth in the money supply. Further, a contraction in economic activity is always accompanied by a similar
contraction of the money supply.

It seems obvious that this should be so, and indeed Hixson points out that the philosopher, David Hume, and his 18th
century colleague, Adam Smith, both expressed this view.
However, Hixson identifies a number of instances in which
prominent past economists have suggested otherwise. He
also notes in the writings of other prominent economists a
lack of recognition of the singular importance of this fundamental connection to an understanding of the workings of an
economy. Hixson's conclusion seems irrefutable.

"Money-supply increases are absolutely essential if aggregate demand is to increase and to be of such a size that the national product can be sold and profits can be realized and if the national product is to increase from year to year. Money is better thought of not as grease on the bearings of an engine but as the fuel without which the engine will not run at all."

Where does this increase in the money supply come from? In accordance with the fractional reserve system, as described earlier, commercial banks create most of this money by loaning into existence money that previously did not exist.

However, the realization that all such money enters the economy as "debt" and that this fact is also of fundamental significance to the workings of an economy has largely escaped the attention of professional economists.

That this is the case is amply illustrated by the oft-repeated mantra of the past that personal savings rates in the United States were too low and needed to be encouraged in order to support private investment, or that government borrowing crowded out borrowing by the private sector. Such statements totally ignore the fact that although savings represent one source of funds for investment, new money created by banks and distributed as loans to businesses or the general public is a much larger and more readily available source of investment funding.

Also the oft-repeated mantra that government debt is too high and needs to be reduced fails to recognize that this would shrink the money supply and create a recession. To avoid this, private debt would need to increase at the same rate that government debt was reduced, thus preventing this decline in the money supply. This, however, is a highly unlikely scenario.

Hixson emphasizes the importance of the connection between growth in the money supply and growth in debt.

That the economy is structured in such a way that growth and prosperity depend almost totally upon our going into debt to banks for the money they create is a fact of monumental importance to an understanding of how the economy works and why it sometimes does not work acceptably well."

In an extraordinary compilation and analysis of available but rarely studied economic data, Hixson proceeds to account for the economic events of recent historical memory – from 1918 through 1987. Throughout, the explanatory importance of the above twin themes of the essential need for the money supply to expand and the fact that the mechanism for doing so ties new money to debt, is made spectacularly evident.

Stripped of many relevant details, the bare-boned outcome of the Hixson analysis is that so long as the new money feeding into the economy is tied to debt, periods of economic prosperity will necessarily be followed by periods of economic contraction and recession. This is because periods of prosperity are necessarily periods when the expansion of the money supply is most vigorous. It is also a period when interest rates are most favorable and debt growth is most vigorous. As the period of prosperity matures the tendency is for interest rates to rise and debt to grow more burdensome.

Unfortunately because of its links to the money supply,

when debt is cancelled through repayment or bankruptcy, a leveraged contraction of the money supply occurs. This contraction accelerates a decline in economic activity that leads to a recessionary period in which the debt load in the economy is reduced to acceptable levels. The above cycle then repeats itself. Economists label this the "business cycle".

The severity of periods of debt readjustment was significantly reduced after the catastrophic experience of the 1929 stock market crash and the ensuing Great Depression. Government involvement in the economy proved necessary. The exclusively private sector economy of the laissez-faire era ended at that time, replaced by the growth of the mixed (private-public sector) economy.

The major monetary change was simply that instead of the growth in private debt being the sole driving force increasing the money supply, now government debt could also be used. Government borrowing and spending could be used to prevent the collapse of the money supply during inevitable periods of private debt readjustment.

This picture properly focuses attention again on the manner in which money is created. That is, private banks do so by creating new deposits by lending out money based on maintaining a reserve of cash in their vaults or on deposit at a Federal reserve bank of a size determined by the Federal Reserve Board (Fed).

The Fed can thus control the money supply by deciding when and how much new cash to inject into the system by open market purchases of government securities. Once this money flows into the private banking system the banks' cash reserves exceed the minimum reserve requirements and these banks are free to increase their loan portfolios by themselves creating new money.

Currently the reserve requirements are such that for every dollar of new money introduced by the Fed, banks are entitled to create more than $10 of new money by making new loans.

The question that flows from Hixson's analysis is why does government create only a small fraction of the new money required by the economy rather than a much larger fraction or even all of it? After all, section 8 of the constitution of the United States gives to the federal government the *"power to coin money and regulate the value thereof"*, while Section 10 specifically prohibits any state from doing so. There can be no doubt, therefore, that the Federal government has the sole legal right and power to create money.

Why then does the federal government not spend into existence money needed to support an expanding economy, rather than borrowing money for government expenditures that they have authorized banks to create. Why do they become indebted to banks by deficit financing when they have the legal right to spend this money simply by writing the checks that produce the increases in new money required by the economy?

This important question is nowhere on the public agenda. More significantly, it is of no apparent concern to the economics profession in general or to academic economists in particular. This is attested to by the fact that any discussion of government spending by professional economists absolutely implies that such spending must be financed by general taxation or by government borrowing.

Period.

The fact, although indisputable, that government spending could be financed by spending into existence the new money necessary to increase the money supply needed to sustain a healthy economy is simply never mentioned. Hixson comments upon this situation as follows.

"An individual who spends in excess of income must necessarily go into debt assuming no inheritance or gifts. Quite to the contrary, a sovereign government that spends in excess of income (taxes) need not necessarily go into debt because such a government can legally create money. Federal spending in excess of taxes may be financed in either of two ways – by deficit spending or by federal creation of money. Dealing with the matter in a way that fails to make the two alternatives crystal clear is unacceptable."

Why then do economists, journalists and legislators make no mention of what according to Hixson should be made crystal clear? Why do they not, Hixson wonders, answer the following questions?

"Why should the government allow banks to create money and then borrow it from them instead of creating the money itself? Since money created by banks puts into circulation money that tends to vanish in a crisis like that of 1929-1933, while money created by government puts into circulation a

non-vanishing sort of money, why should not the latter be greatly preferred over the former?

Why, if the money creation process is 'too fraught with peril for it to be put in the hands of government bureaucrats,' is there less peril in putting it into the hands of the bureaucrats of private banks?

Why, granting for the sake of argument the oft made but false assertion that 'money creation always causes price inflation,' is there any reason to suppose that money created by governments is more inflationary than money created by banks?"

Strangely enough, as Hixson documents, during the Great Depression such questions were on the minds of academic economists in the U.S. as witnessed in economic publications of that period by Irving Fisher of Yale, John Commons of the University of Wisconsin, and Henry Simons of the University of Chicago.

However, this inquisitiveness disappeared once the prescription of the most influential economist of that time, John Maynard Keynes became standard orthodoxy. In his publication, *General Theory of Employment, Interest and Money*, he proposed that governments should borrow and spend money into the economy as the best means to restore the money supply.

An important consequence of placing money creation almost exclusively in the hands of the private financial sector has been the growth of what Hixson describes as the "casino" economy.

This means the amount of speculative money entering the economy through the financial system has grown well beyond that required to ensure that financial markets function effectively. These are comparable to the activities supported by gambling casinos. This excess money, circulating around the financial system, creates no further benefits for the productive sector of the economy, even though such benefits are supposed to be the "raison d'être" of the financial system.

It accounts for the fact (2013) that Wall Street has fully recovered from the effects of the "Great Recession", while Main Street lags far behind. The near zero interest rates encourages the money that the Fed has been feeding into the financial system by its policy of "quantitative easing" to preferentially support speculation in the financial markets rather than to provide loans to support productive enterprise.

From statistics mined from the government publications identified earlier, Hixson shows that from 1947 to 1987 the industrial sector grew by a factor of 14. The financial sector, however, grew at more than twice this rate, going from less than 20% the size of the industrial sector in 1947 to almost 50% by 1990.

Over this same period the population of the U.S. nearly doubled. The agricultural sector of the economy not only provided the food for this large population increase, but also created the surplus used to feed other country's populations. The result in financial terms was that farm income increased over this period by 203%. By contrast the financial sector over the same period increased its real income by almost 5000%. One is left to speculate as to the societal contribution of this spectacular increase.

The continuation of the trends identified by Hixson some twenty years ago, further aided by the ongoing deregulation of the banking system, has resulted increasingly in the money creation entrusted to the financial sector being diverted into speculative finance. This has been responsible for the growth of the casino economy, made spectacularly evident with the dramatic collapse of the financial system in 2008. Equally spectacular was the complete absence of any whiff of concern in the economic community as to the role played by the current mode of money creation in fomenting this disaster.

The outcome of my associations with the ideas and studies of Bill Krehm and Bill Hixson reviewed from the perspective of my thoughts on scientific thinking are illuminating. A critical part of scientific thinking is a willingness to accept the importance of giving to adverse data (those subversive of current beliefs) their proper due, and, when necessary, willingly abandoning long-held and perhaps cherished perspectives. To whatever extent these characteristics existed, they disappeared from the field of economic studies sometime during the 1930s. They have been spectacularly absent ever since.

Thus, we see that the adverse data implied from any careful analysis of the root causes of the Great Depression, and set forth in the writings of such as Fisher, Commons and Simons, then more recently by Hixson, have been totally ignored.

This is also true of the adverse data relating to general equilibrium theory as set forth by Krehm. In both instances the economics profession has been unable or unwilling to abandon its cherished beliefs. As a result, we all suffer the consequences when seriously flawed economic thinking is the basis by which national governments seek to sustain prosperity in the economy and to finance their own operations.

Nothing speaks to this more eloquently than the 2008 collapse of the economy, the current (2013) economic malaise here, in Europe and elsewhere and the chaos and confusion of the public debate as to suitable remedies.

A goal fundamental to the evolutionary progress of our species, as suggested earlier, is to organize an economy so that opportunities are maximized for each and every one of us to most productively contribute to the ongoing and future benefit of our societies.

Achieving this goal means that the productivity "potential" of a society – the summation of all productive energies available from its citizenry at any given time – be fully realized. One requirement for this to happen, as made clear by Hixson, is that the money supply in the economy be sufficient to support this level of productivity.

The manner by which the money supply is currently created by the private sector has amply demonstrated frequent failures to sustain this desirable balance. This failure, a problem important to general wellbeing, is largely overlooked.

We have somehow concluded that it is the availability of money not the availability of productive capacity that establishes a ceiling on what can be achieved. We lack the economic literacy to appreciate that what we can and cannot do as a nation depends only on how well we engage the energies and skills of our people. What we lack is an understanding as to how an economic system should function so as to ensure that the money supply is adequate to achieve this goal.

With this in mind, consider how our economy might function if the ideas championed by Krehm and Hixson were given proper credence. First, consider Hixson's ideas about money creation.

Recent events strongly support Hixson's view that the time has come to question the current means by which the Federal government out-sources the creation of new money to the private financial sector through the fractional reserve system.

The alternative approach recommended by Hixson would have an agency of the Federal government (e.g. the Federal Reserve) authorize for direct government use, more or even all of the new money technically required to sustain healthy activity in the economy. This would reduce or eliminate the role of the financial sector in the money creation business.

They would otherwise continue their essential role in ensuring the ready flow and distribution of the money supply to meet the purchase demands, loan requests and investment preferences in the economy at large, as they currently do. But this would then be based on their ability to attract deposits from both businesses and the general public through the quality of their services and investment offerings, not as a free gift from the federal government.

The fractional reserve system would in this way be replaced by a federal government "investment" spending program approved by Congress, designed to annually spend into existence the amount of new money needed to maintain a healthy economy as determined and authorized through a technical assessment conducted by the Federal Reserve or some other government agency.

The obvious advantages of this alternative system are first, that the current connection of the money supply to bank debt would be severed. This would prevent the contractions of the money supply during economic downturns that accentuate and feed economic recessions.

Second, this form of money creation would be a source of badly needed public sector investment. This is unrecognized by current economic expertise that insists government spending can be financed only by taxation or borrowing.

Finally, government creation of money would reduce or eliminate deficit spending and thus reduce the interest payments that constitute that insidious flow of taxpayer money into the financial sector that inevitably accentuates the growth of the "casino" economy.

Money creation, by these arguments, should be high on the current economic reassessment agenda seeking to revive our economy. Are there any fundamental, rather than historical or ideological reasons for retaining a fractional reserve system in its present highly leveraged form? Would it not be better to eliminate it entirely in favor of a government money creation system? Or could a case be made for some mixture of the two as working best – partial government and partial (de-leveraged) fractional reserve system?

The uproar from the financial community should any serious suggestion emerge that their milch cow (the fractional reserve system) be reduced or eliminated would inevitably focus on the dire consequences of an uncontrolled government printing press. Historical examples whereby this process has debauched the currency would be used to imply inevitability. However, only the arrogance of ignorance can proclaim that money needed by a healthy economy and created by government is necessarily inflationary while the same amount of money created by banks is not.

A structural approach for the Federal spending that injects new money into the economy could well be based on a rational business model. Federal spending currently has no categorical distinctions. The normal political process could be used to codify this spending into current and non-current spending. Current spending would be analogous to those IRS approved expenses found on the profit and loss statement of any business. Non-current spending would be associated with depreciable assets appearing on a typical business balance sheet.

For instance, payment for social security, unemployment insurance, food stamps, some medical costs etc., could be codified as current spending. Money spent for infrastructure – roads, railways, buildings, etc. – could be codified as non-current expenses. This could also apply to money spent to protect or enhance the environment, to combat global warming, to promote basic, industrial and medical research, to enhance preventive aspects of health care, to educate the next generation, etc.

The codification of many items of spending, such as those related to the environment, education, and research areas, etc., might prove controversial. Ultimately, however, a codification procedure could be put in place by which any federal spending would fall into one or other of these two categories.

Current government spending could logically be financed through taxation. Non-current spending could be financed by new money creation. This government created new money would be restrained by law for non-current spending, and given priority in terms of maximizing the public good, as determined by normal political debate.

Once money creation became a technical responsibility of the Federal government, the financial sector would need substantial realignment. Recent events have shown the dire consequences of allowing the consolidation of the separate pillars of the financial sector in large corporations deemed "too big to fail". Returning to the reforms that followed the Great Depression of the 1930s whereby these pillars of the financial sector, commercial banking, investment banking (stock brokerage), mortgage banking, and insurance were separated, would reduce the size of corporations below the "too big to fail" level.

Such reforms would also better ensure that the capital reserves needed to support each of these activities would remain healthy and not be merged into a common pool.

Additionally, as the money supply is not preferentially directed to the financial sector by the government, but rather flows from the personal preferences of millions of individuals and businesses, a more rational financial system would emerge. The result would minimize the casino aspects of the financial system and more directly connect it to supporting productive enterprise.

The second gulf that separates current economic thinking from the real world has to do with the question of price stability. As already indicated, current economic dogma sees price as determined solely by the relative strength of supply and demand in the marketplace. Stability is sought by adjusting interest rates to combat any excessive imbalance in one direction or the other.

Businesses in the real world look at price quite differently – through the logic of the accounting process. Price, accordingly, is a logical outcome of identifying costs and adding them up. Price increases come about because of increases in one or more of such costs as raw materials, salaries and wages, departmental costs, insurance, accounting and legal costs, interest on debt, other overheads, taxes, and profit.

What happens to these costs is the logical consequence of the pricing environment. This is defined not only by the current supply-demand situation in the economy; non-market forces are also influential.

Examples of this are the level of direct and indirect taxation, increases in medical insurance costs, the extent to which increasing litigation raises liability insurance premiums, the interest rate on debt as set by the Federal Reserve, plus costs associated with meeting federal and state regulation with respect to safety in the workplace, employment and employee relations, and the environment.

What needs to be understood is that the supply-demand relationship in the marketplace is only part of the story. What must be added are the non-market forces, such as those identified above, that also factor into the price equation. Economists, in general, are blind to these non-market forces.

Any businessman knows that when governments increase taxes or licensing fees, or introduce costly regulations, or medical insurance rates increase, or trial lawyers up the cost of liability insurance, or banks increase interest rates, that the costs to produce and deliver goods and services go up.

If such costs cannot realistically be absorbed in the item called profit, then of course a general price rise will occur which obviously is independent of the supply-demand situation in the economy. In fact such price increases themselves will drive the supply-demand relationship, rather than the other way around.

This monumental difference distinguishing reality from the current price dogma requires a new approach to the question of price stability. The response dictated by current dogma, is to view any increase in the consumer price index as meaning, unequivocally, too much demand in the economy, and only one solution, an increase in interest rates. The consequence is necessarily "knee jerk", not analytical.

A more reliable and desirable response is to analyze economic data to determine the extent to which the unpriced, non-market factors highlighted earlier are putting upward pressure on prices. The appropriate action thus depends on the analysis and could take many forms. The least likely based on current evidence would be to increase interest rates, since obviously an increase in interest rates automatically increases one of the basic cost pressures feeding further price increases.

By following the dictates of what any serious scientific thought would label as a very questionable economic model, all western governments have damaged their economies. They have inadvertently promoted the casino aspects of their economies to the detriment of the productive aspects. This has currently created needless hardships, not limited only to their own peoples, but affecting all populations around the world.

Much is yet to be learned about the proper role of the public sector in promoting stable and prosperous economies. Of first importance is to ensure that the economic model by which to assess available public options is a sound one, subject to careful scientific scrutiny. Failing this, making effective public policy is well nigh impossible.

Current proposals, whether left wing tax increases or right wing spending cuts, will prove as equally unsuccessful as their predecessors.

Our economic system functioning in its current fashion is a major obstacle to overcome in setting our species on a more successful evolutionary pathway.

Chapter V

*B*usiness

An economy that makes available a wide range of goods and services is essential to our current survival and wellbeing. From such offerings we select and purchase what best satisfies our needs and wants. Businesses provide these goods and services. The greater their number and diversity and the better the quality of their products at "best" prices, the greater will be our prosperity and wellbeing.

Businesses that deliver such products will necessarily earn the wherewithal to continue their operations. This means that "profit" is a natural by-product of meeting the above-stated business goals that best promote the evolutionary success of our species.

Nevertheless, standard business education teaches something quite different. It states, unequivocally, that the primary purpose of a business is to "make money". This view is widely held, not only within the business community, but also throughout society. Nevertheless, conceptually, according to the above logic, it is a philosophic error.

The development of widely affordable consumer products was an outcome of the scientific and industrial revolutions. Mass production in the manufacture and sale of such products was the required means to achieve affordable prices. The public corporation was the solution to securing the large initial capital requirements needed by such businesses. Thousands or millions of small investors through the purchase of its common shares widely distributed the risk.

Successful stock sales, however, demanded the promise of rich rewards. For the public corporation to meet such promises meant maximizing growth in order to maximize revenues and profits. The financial system that evolved to support public corporations naturally valued their shares exclusively on their current profitability and the prospect for increasing revenues that attend growth in size. Thus "making money" came to be understood as the dominant purpose of businesses.

Planning how revenues are to be increased is far more certain when focused on the short term. Also public corporations reward senior management exclusively on short-term results. Potential adverse longer-term consequences thus pale in significance compared to perceived short-term gains. What we have experienced over the past several decades is the predictable outcome of an economy dominated by large businesses with a primary focus on "making money".

In America over these decades we have seen the collapse into bankruptcy, followed mostly by government bailouts of one sort or another, of most large airline companies, most large automobile companies, some large energy companies, many large banks, S&L corporations and other financial houses. In all these cases, management decisions that "made money" in the short term had devastating longer-term consequences.

The history of many large corporations follows a common path. They come into being based on an innovative product concept. They grow larger, first to meet the demand for the new innovative product, then through acquisitions to meet the demands of the financial community to make more money. Rarely thereafter do they ever show anything like the innovative capability that brought them into existence. The focus on short-term profitability and growth takes over. Frequently, as an eventual outcome, they become moribund.

Another inevitable consequence of large business growth is that management acquires increasing power. This accretion of power inevitably brings with it corrupting temptations. This is evidenced by the ever more frequent legal prosecution for corporate wrongdoing and of senior executives for egregious actions.

Such are merely the extremes of the more modest corrupting influences that affect behavioral patterns. These can become quite pervasive throughout corporate management and affect the actions of their employees. In the name of the corporation and making money, people can find themselves supporting or taking actions of a character they would rarely contemplate in any purely personal interactions.

Think of the prelude to the 2008 financial collapse – the many high risk, sub-prime mortgages that actual sales people, encouraged by corporate management, enticed customers to accept for home purchases they could ill afford. Another illustration is the recently highlighted, "blind eye" approach of large corporate retailers to employee safety and other deficit conditions in manufacturing operations in third world countries, fostered by the pressure of their demands for low cost goods.

Such behavior is magnified at senior management levels by government regulation. This allows purely legal considerations to obscure and replace moral judgments. Whatever isn't prohibited by a careful analysis of the letter of regulatory law become acceptable practices for large corporate entities.

A new means to "make more money" need only be cleared by lawyers to be put into effect: e.g. a money-saving procedure with some potential environmental or safety implications, a new tax avoidance scheme, etc.

The growth of an alternative approach to business operations that would automatically discourage these socially undesirable outcomes would be beneficial to our evolutionary progress. Advances in technology now make such an alternative conceivable.

Small privately owned businesses are not required by their ownership structure to follow the philosophic error responsible for the above cited outcomes. They have the freedom to focus primary attention, not specifically on making money, but rather on the achievement of excellence in most efficiently delivering the highest quality products as the means to best satisfy customer needs and wants.

A successful outcome in pursuit of these goals ensures the earnings required to allow continuing operations. Making money thereby becomes the "by-product", rather than the "purpose" of such businesses. Seeking to ensure the success of their small business over a lifetime also ensures the incentive for longer term planning.

The current dominance of large businesses is based on economies of size. Yet over the past several decades advances in computer technology, in robotics, and by the communications revolution have made affordable to small businesses automation and efficiency options previously only accessible to large corporations.

This accelerating erosion in economies of size increasingly exposes the largely overlooked, but surprisingly low ceiling that severely limits a large corporation's ability to achieve high levels of internal operational efficiencies.

The primary challenge of management in large corporations concerns the organizing and managing of the large numbers of employees required to conduct the activities of the business. A hierarchical management structure is needed. Well defined job descriptions, fixed pay scales, detailed employee manuals, etc., are required at all levels. Also the road to promotion can create a highly politicized environment.

Most of the workers in such organizations do what their managers tell them to do with no thought as to whether there might be better ways to do things. Managers seeking to move up the hierarchy tend to function in ways that will most effectively advance their careers. At times these could well be at odds with what would best advance the interests of their company. Workers or managers who act contrary to these "unwritten rules" are rarely rewarded and mostly are, openly or inadvertently, discouraged from pursuing any such actions.

These structural realities mean that very few people in the organization are focused on finding a better way to do the job of creating the highest quality product in the most efficient manner possible. Most people are quite satisfied with a comfortable status quo.

The consequences are obvious to anyone like myself who has spent a business lifetime visiting and working with clients and customers in large corporations. Significant inefficiencies are readily encountered and easily observable; e.g. the frequency with which people can be observed "off task", contacts referring to the time "wasted" in meetings, lower level employees expressing frustration with management who won't listen to them, time wasted waiting for a union person to affect simple repairs that others are not allowed to do, and so on.

Large businesses have access to readily available sources of money through their own cash flows and through easily attainable loans from banks and other financial institutions. This promotes a simple logic. All problems can best be resolved by throwing money at them. This, together with the importance that accrues to a manager's profile when their departments expand, means that hiring more employees is an automatic response to almost all such problems. Most large companies thereby end up over-employing, explaining why when market conditions deteriorate they can make the regularly observed, draconian layoffs. What disappears once money is readily available is any deep thought as to how far less costly alternative solutions might be conceived.

The reality is that large companies, to function at all, have had to accept surprisingly low ceilings on labor productivity and overall efficiency. Until recently these have been more than offset by economies of size. Now things are changing.

Small businesses lack the structural problems that face large businesses. This gives them the potential to achieve levels of operational efficiency well above those attainable by large corporations. Such cost benefits when fully exploited by small businesses, aided by the manner in which new technologies are eliminating factors determining economies of size, could well drive the economy to reach a cross over point where small privately owned businesses can begin to competitively challenge large public corporations. Over time this could extend to more and more sectors of the economy. The outcome could then become a clear division in the economy between an expanding and properly recognized and supported small business sector and a contracting large business sector occupied only by those businesses whose large size is "actually" rather than "assumed" to be essential to their competitiveness.

Our society has developed the private sector infrastructure to promote, and support only the growth and wellbeing of the large business sector. This sector includes all publicly traded corporations and those businesses planning to go public. The country's many schools of business focus their attention exclusively on the operations of companies in this sector of the economy. They educate and train their students to become the future managers and executives of public corporations.

Angel investors and venture capitalists have come to function within the financial community to provide capital for those start-up businesses that will seek to become public corporations. The former provide the seed capital, the latter the growth capital. Together this carries successful start-ups to the point where another fixture of the financial industry, the investment banker, takes over and manages the initial public offering (IPO). This converts the wannabe into full membership in the capitalist system. This requires accepting the single, universal and necessary goal of bending all efforts to grow larger and make more money so as to increase the share value of the corporation as far as possible beyond the value of its IPO.

The small business sector, as I define it, includes only those privately owned businesses managed and operated by their owners with no intention of going public. Such businesses can maintain the advantages of being small only by placing limits on their growth. This will effectively mean that the lowest paid employee will rarely be more than one management level and certainly not more than two management levels distant from the owner.

Currently small businesses, so defined, have no reliable, well-recognized private sector (i.e. non-governmental) infrastructure whatsoever to support their operations. Governments have come to see these small businesses as being an important, but disadvantaged part of one universal business sector, rather than as a member of a potentially viable alternative and distinctive small business sector.

Taxpayer dollars are thus enlisted to encourage and fund them. This is done through the federal Small Business Administration (SBA) with their guaranteed loan programs or through other programs funded by the SBA or state governments. These fund SCORE and its free consulting programs staffed by retired executives (usually from large businesses), and countless other non-profit, free educational offerings and special loan funds that typically promote a mode of small business operation based on conventional concepts and practices really appropriate only to large corporations.

Such educational emphasis disadvantages the small business recipients of this largess. This inhibits the growth of the vibrant small business sector postulated above and undermines the growth of the private sector infrastructure needed to support and enhance such growth.

These arguments suggest that historical necessity has led us down a particular evolutionary path to an economy that functions in such a way as to exclusively promote and support the dominant position held by large public corporations. Small privately owned businesses receive no such private sector support.

The evidence presented above is pointing ever more strongly to the conclusion that this evolutionary pathway has been in response to historical conditions that no longer persist. It is now feasible to focus on developing the private sector institutional infrastructure needed to support the growth of a small business sector capable of providing a competitive challenge to the large business sector. This could help shift our societies onto a new and potentially more successful evolutionary track by which to produce and distribute the goods and services so essential to our wellbeing.

What private sector institutional support structures are needed to promote the growth of a small business sector capable of competing for dominance with large corporations in many sectors of the economy?

My professional lifetime has been immersed in the operation of my own small businesses while dealing primarily with clients and customers in the large business sector. This has led me to an understanding that practices I had come to embrace empirically had very fundamental reasons supporting their value. But, as such, they were feasible only because mine was a "small" operation.

Recounting the experiences that have led to these conclusions is the best way to illuminate the kind of private sector institutional structures I believe are needed to support the development of a vibrant small business sector – one capable of providing a competitive challenge to the large business sector and thereby shifting societal evolution in a more promising direction.

Of first and crucial importance is to provide an alternative business education based on the study of small business operations, not as miniature large businesses, but as an entirely different species.

When I started my first small business in Montreal as a research and development consultant to the pulp, paper and allied industries, I attended a number of courses given at the McGill University School of Business. I learned many interesting things. Retrospectively, however, I realized that much of what I'd learned was of little relevance to my subsequent business activities. Throughout my career I have repeatedly found this to be the case when studying the business literature or attending business courses. This would, of course, not have been the case had I chosen to work for a large corporation.

Business literature and courses flow from the academic study of large businesses. The result is that few of these ideas are directly applicable to a small business operation. They frequently are tangential rather than central to such an understanding. Until acquiring some substantial acquaintance with the operational realities of a small business, and thus having a basis for judging what may be relevant, typical business education is in many ways more of a distraction than a benefit.

To illustrate this, consider the following areas of business education where the emphasis relates specifically to the way large businesses operate, in contrast to practices more appropriate to the running of small businesses.

Consider marketing. Large businesses, driven by the need to attract large numbers of customers, have developed a sophisticated approach by which large advertising budgets seek to embed in consumers a persuasive message that will impact on their purchase decisions. Marketing means creating and communicating a "perception" of a product in the minds of an anonymous public that proves to correlate with sales success. This perception rarely has any strong connection to the reality of the product. It is frequently more gimmick than truth.

Small businesses can survive happily with far fewer customers. Prospects are thus more easily targeted. I found that properly understanding, articulating and communicating the realities of my business and its offerings became the essential challenge, rather than looking for clever ways to create a "perception" of some anonymous presence. This focused my attention on building business and product "reputation" rather than product "branding". Small business marketing, from my perspective, had a completely different focus than that promoted by conventional marketing literature and courses.

Consider accounting and financial management. Large businesses have huge numbers of financial transactions that flow into complex accounting systems. From these, managers and their executives are provided standardized reports showing how well the company is functioning both in respect to senior management expectations and in comparison to industry norms and the performance of competitors.

It is the only means by which top executives can make any sense whatsoever of the activities of the businesses they manage. It is the primary means to assess the performance of lower level management.

Another requirement is to allow skilled company accountants to adjust and publish financial statements for its shareholders and the financial markets that support the best possible financial image of the company. This activity is widely acknowledged as "creative" accounting. These aspects of financial management have no relevance whatsoever for a small privately owned business.

When time-share computer capability first became available, my entrepreneurial activities required a very careful review of how this new resource could best be used to handle the accounting and financial data for a small business operation such as mine. I wanted to look beyond the routine requirement to supply bankers and the IRS with accurate financial data.

I quickly realized that in contrast to large businesses, my involvement in day-to-day activities was such that I already knew a great deal about operations without any need to consult a financial statement.

Ulultimately I realized that the primary value to me of computer accounting was to make feasible a new approach to planning. This consisted of seeing my business as being driven by a series of experiments, each experiment, based on its outcome, leading to the next experiment, in a never ending logical sequence.

These experiments were conceived as specific ways to test out new ideas for increasing sales, or reducing costs. Using computers, such experiments could be framed in quantitative terms by projecting the improved outcomes predicted to result from implementing these new ideas. Every experiment meant creating the accounting structure that would properly accumulate all expense and revenue data relevant to the experiment. In this way, by reviewing computer generated financial reports, actual results could be easily and readily compared periodically to predicted outcomes.

This knowledge allowed rapid assessments as to the value of new ideas, allowing them to be strengthened or abandoned in a timely fashion. Such an approach in the absence of computers was impossibly time-consuming.

So it turns out that what small business people need by way of financial management training is quite different than what is required by those who manage large businesses. Small business accounting is relatively simple and can be successfully taught without getting into many areas of accounting needed only in large corporations. The basic form of financial statements to satisfy banks and the IRS can be easily grasped.

The most important feature, however, is to understand the planning process based on conceiving and testing out experiments. This requires a particular understanding and approach to budgeting and the use of a simple but flexible accounting system. This specific training is not central and exclusive to financial management courses in a normal business degree.

Consider human resource management. Large companies have a separate human resources department responsible for creating the rules within which large numbers of employees can most successfully function. These rules and the outcomes they produce are studied and become the fodder for business education in this area. Much that is presented, while having some general conceptual value, is clearly geared to problems dealing with large numbers of employees.

As I grew experienced, I found it best to collaborate with each employee individually, to create what essentially was the best work environment to encourage that individual to become most productive in helping to achieve the goals I set for the business. This is a far different challenge with far reaching consequences, simply not feasible to pursue in large companies, and therefore not a subject for discussion in normal business courses.

Consider the role of management. Large companies are organized with a hierarchical structure. Senior managers impose rules and define profit goals, while middle and junior managers work, as best they can, to impress senior management with outcomes in accordance with these rules and goals.

This system establishes the role of manager as someone who is primarily concerned with planning, instructing others what to do, and maintaining oversight that all is going according to senior management plans.

All of this, of course, is driven by the bottom line mentality of maximizing current profit. Business education flows from the study of how best to make this complex management system function most effectively. Again, to a small business owner little of this is relevant.

Small businesses lack the size and resources to contemplate having managers with no other responsibilities. In fact such other responsibilities because of their importance to daily operations tend to have priority. In my experience as a small business owner, my management time was best spent ensuring that every employee developed as far as possible a self-managing capability requiring the least oversight from me. This required that they come to fully understand both their own role in the operation and how it fit with everyone else's. Remuneration could then be linked to how well they accomplished this.

Another management concept I found essential to achieving my goals was to identify which operational functions of my business were "core" functions. Careful analysis was required to identify substantive reasons why certain functions absolutely needed to be performed either by myself or by my employees. That is, they needed to be performed in-house, thus defining them as "core" functions.

All others, for which such an argument could not be sustained, were to be considered non-core functions. As my business developed and demands on my time or that of my employees became excessive, the first option was always to regain time by outsourcing non-core functions rather than by increasing employment.

This established the principle that people in my business focused as much as possible on becoming ever better at discharging core functions. From a managerial perspective I sought to ensure that all non-core functions were efficiently outsourced as soon as could be afforded, to businesses whose execution of these tasks was their core function. These management practices are not common in large businesses and so are largely outside the purview of normal business education.

It took me many years of trial and error and much subsequent analytic thinking to identify all the practices, some of which are discussed above, that I now recognize were important to the successful running of my own businesses. Small businesses need the kind of business education that promotes these concepts and practices in some acceptable institutional form. Relying on the uncertain consequences of the school of hard knocks is not the way to prepare businesses to best contribute to a successful economy.

After business education, the second important role for a small business private sector support infrastructure is to facilitate the formation of small business collaboratives. One of the continual problems I faced in developing my businesses was how to acquire services I lacked the experience or knowledge to provide, and couldn't afford to employ or to engage through an outside consultant.

An early experience during my consulting years came while talking to a marketing consultant engaged by one of my own clients. In chatting with him about my business he was persuasive regarding his abilities to help me. I suggested that if he were that confident he should be prepared to execute the project on the basis of receiving an enhanced payment but only after it proved successful in securing me a client engagement. Somewhat to my surprise he agreed to do so, and so we collaborated in a program that accomplished this outcome.

Later I was faced with a project requiring computer technology to improve the performance of one of the instruments we had developed. I could not afford the consulting fees to acquire the necessary know-how.

Remembering my earlier experience I began to chat with potential suppliers of this technology about a royalty arrangement on sales of a successfully developed instrument as an alternative to normal billings. The eventual outcome was exactly such an agreement with a professor of electrical engineering at a local university. Thus began a mutually successful and close collaboration over many years. This may seem to some as merely a form of subcontracting. However the extent to which risks and rewards are shared is not a normal feature of subcontracting. That is why I use the term collaboratives.

Other experiences from my business development reinforced this concept of the value of collaboratives.

In the development of a particular instrument, I needed to work out the exact manner in which to achieve unusually precise tolerances in assembling component parts. This required designing special jigs to be used during machining as the only means to attain such tolerances. I rented time in a local machine shop to prove out these details, but recognized that the demands of this approach required more skill than this particular shop could guarantee. So with the final designs complete I approached a large aerospace company in Montreal about producing this unit.

In my discussions with the contact person I identified the precision requirements and offered to show how I had achieved them. He indicated that the very tight tolerances required by the aerospace industry made them experts in the area and thus airily dismissed my suggestion.

When the first unit was rejected as having failed to meet the designated tolerances, I was visited by a delegation from the company including the original contact person. I showed them the clear evidence for the failure, and as the others were discussing what to do, the original contact person drew me aside. He remembered my earlier suggestion and now asked to be filled in.

Thereafter, the units they produced met specifications and all was well until later when the delivery of a particular order was delayed, then delayed again and again. This finally elicited the explanation that "Joe was sick." It turned out that Joe was an old-timer, a skilled machinist to whom they had turned over my information and who was responsible for producing our units. The problem was that no one else in this large organization could duplicate what Joe could do. And, Joe was over 80 years old!

In connection with another project I had met a Serbian machinist trained in Germany and Switzerland who had recently started his own machine shop. Faced with the above dilemma, I approached him about making this tester, taking our prototype down for him to examine. He assured me he would have no trouble meeting my specifications. And he didn't.

Thus began a collaboration and friendship that has persisted over the years. We discussed ways in which we, by prepaying for raw materials, could allow him to use slow periods to build our equipment as inventory, without him having to finance the necessary material purchases. Final payment was made only on delivery after we received an order. To make this work we guaranteed the purchase of some minimum number of units annually. He made valuable pricing concessions in response to the flexibility and support we provided. On this basis he built up inventory on our behalf to suit his own work-flow. In this way we were able to minimize our delivery times to our customers and be assured that spare parts would be instantly available when needed.

He helped with prototype design in development projects and produced prototypes at cost of materials and labor only. He was quite happy to take on the risk of making profits only from future sales of a final unit. In effect he became an unofficial partner, sharing risk and rewards in our endeavors and ever available at no direct cost to work with us in solving problems.

He further provided us with a totally reliable manufacturing capability. This was far superior to anything that we could have built and managed ourselves. At no time did we ever consider the benefits of capturing the manufacturing profit, even when our sales volume had increased to a level where this might have been a temptation.

My business followed the typical path of engaging commissioned sales people to generate and service sales in various geographic areas. I came to realize that the skill of such sales agents lay in their ability to persuade potential customers that the product they represented was the best of the available options to meet a need the prospect already recognized.

Novel equipment, such as ours, needed to be introduced to prospective customers in a very different manner. The prospective customer had to be persuaded that our equipment actually met an important need of which the prospect was initially ignorant. Sales reps, I discovered, typically lacked an understanding as to how this could best be accomplished.

Thus to effectively use sales reps to sell our "new" instruments required that we develop a relationship completely different from the norm that connected them to the other businesses they served. They needed to see my business as being different from the norm, to see its challenge as introducing potential customers to a new and unfamiliar technology. This required a different sales approach, and to make it work, a different sales agreement.

It meant developing an agreed approach to working "together" to manage the time the agent was to devote to our products, and how such time was to be spent. What was needed was a collaboration reflected in the sales agreement.

To make this work we not only offered a better than normal commission rate, but also gave unusual guarantees to protect against arbitrary termination. This commonly occurs when a commissioned sales person is too successful and can be replaced by an in-house salesperson at lower cost. Introducing and making these collaborations work was not an easy task, but enough were successful to prove their value.

As volume of sales increased we reached a point at which we felt the need to "outsource" the creative (rather than technical) side of our marketing effort. I decided to seek a marketing group who would consider the idea of a collaboration whereby they would spend time getting to know all about our products our people and what we were trying to do, for a pre-defined small "honest money" cost to us. This would allow them to identify needs they could satisfy, proposing desirable outcomes and budget requirements.

Of the half dozen or so people we talked to, only one was not completely baffled by the request. Rather his eyes spar-kled at the challenge. It turned out to be quite an amazing collaboration, ultimately embracing coherence and creativity in the design and production of brochures, manuals, sales presentations and then a web site. Over this time we never specifically proposed a project. On a regular basis he would simply drop by and chat. Periodically he would arrive with some sketches and a proposal for doing something along with a budget for us to consider. Rarely were these proposals not immediately endorsed.

These examples of what I term "collaboratives" were, when implemented, simply ways to try and solve specific problems. Only later did I come to see them as fundamental to the way small businesses should operate. I came to visualize many ways beyond my own experiences whereby collaboratives would allow small businesses to prosper in ways impossible without such an approach.

For instance, businesses with complimentary products could form "product-bundling" collaboratives, tailoring their in-dividual products to best "fit" together to bring an enhanced product capability into the marketplace.

Groups of retail businesses could form "ad-bundling" collaborative to share in the cost for creating and displaying local, or Internet advertising.

Small businesses could acquire marketing or financial management support through "sweat equity" collaboratives whereby a service organization could "earn" an equity position only after achieving predefined successful outcomes.

Small business educators need to study and expand on the concept of collaboratives. In this way small businesses will come to automatically study and identify the forms of collaboration that could be beneficial, and the time frame as to when they might best be pursued.

This collaborative approach offers a start-up business planning to proceed in the normal way toward an IPO, a different option – a new development path. On this path, the goal would be to remain a small privately owned business while achieving outcomes in terms of market penetration comparable to those expected from a large public corporation. This requires focusing exclusively on an essential core capability and then "growing" through a network of collaboratives that provide a geographically expanding capability to deliver product.

Let me further explain this important concept. Any start-up company must have, or develop, a marketable product and then demonstrate that this product can secure a market of willing buyers.

These two requirements are successfully demonstrated only when a business achieves break-even; i.e. revenues have grown to equal operational expenses.

Any start up business needs to formulate the plan of action that will accomplish this mission. The conventional approach is to sum up the anticipated costs dictated by this plan and to raise the investment capital to meet such costs. For growth businesses this means finding angel investors to initiate the path toward an IPO.

For small businesses without this growth promise, it's tough sledding, with the likelihood of being under-financed when shoehorned into some kind of government funded or guaranteed loan program.

The Internet and social networks now make feasible a different approach. Think not of money requirements to execute the start-up plan. Rather consider the skill and resource requirements beyond those provided by the founder(s). The individuals or businesses capable of providing for these skills or resources can be researched on the web and then qualified. By use of acceptable equity stakes and creative collaborative arrangements, such sources can be integrated into a viable business. This will reduce initial capital requirements to the rock bottom level that greatly facilitates their acquisition.

The outcome of this approach is a business with the requisite capability to achieve the depth of knowledge and practical experience needed for product and market development.

Market development is focused on a carefully predetermined sales region, maximizing accessibility and limiting size. The goal is to develop the model for a regional business that can successfully deliver and service the new product.

Once this model has been perfected to the level that it can

demonstrate reliable profitability, the business can refocus on two objectives. First is to continue servicing the original region as a "laboratory" for improving both product quality and operational efficiency. This should be the minimum objective for any small business.

For those businesses with obvious growth potential, a second objective is to develop a capability to package the current business model as the basis for developing collaborative business arrangements in other geographical regions. The collaborative agreement visualized is one in which the requisite training allows a collaborative business to most quickly apply the initial business model to any new region with a suitable connection to existing collaborators, on a sales based royalty fee.

Once a business has demonstrated a successful business model, it needs to focus attention on ensuring future improvements to product quality and operational efficiency. This means staying focused on the originating product so as to maintain into the indefinite future its supremacy in the marketplace.

At the same time, the opportunity to replicate marketing and sales success elsewhere is out-sourced to collaboratives. These collaboratives, other businesses operating quite independently with far more freedom than a typical franchisee, can, with a proper training program, be expected to quickly and reliably extend sales.

The result is a "satellite system" business in which the activities of the founding company, supported by the royalty income from satellite businesses, develop the stream of product and process improvements upon which the satellite collaboratives rely for continuing profitability. The satellite businesses, although operating independently, contribute experiences and ideas promoting effective future developments, and thus enhance the family atmosphere that is central to the collaborative concept.

I found that for all the collaborative projects I undertook, identifying potential prospects for collaborative associations was a time consuming problem. Of great benefit, and now quite conceivable, would be an online database identifying collaborative prospects in each collaborative area. It would identify relevant information for those small businesses, consultants and other service providers, professors and so on who would have an interest in participating in any particular form of collaborative. The development of such a database is part of the needed small business infrastructure that I have been describing.

The third, final, and perhaps most difficult part of building the necessary small business infrastructure, is the means by which the private sector is to create a financial support system for small businesses. This would be analogous to that already discussed as available to large corporations.

This could happen in the following manner. Currently people with some surplus money to invest, can do so as an outside investor in the stock market. Their only normal connection to the businesses in which they invest is through their stock price listings and financial reports and proxy forms. An alternative option could develop.

Suppose small privately owned businesses were structured so that their owner(s) received nominal and fixed salaries unchangeable without investor approval. Company profits, so constrained, would be required to first fund a preferred annual dividend payment to outside investors at some agreed-upon rate above an average annual bank interest rate.

This dividend rate could also apply to the owner(s). Any increase to this dividend payment to owners would also apply to the outside investors. Such a business could then become an investment opportunity for a person with useful relevant knowledge and/or experience, who would enjoy opportunities to be involved in helping that business succeed.

The business would form collaborations with its investors who could then be classified as "involved" investors. Each would receive whatever operational information they requested, based on their interests. Owners could seek help or advice at any time through this collaboration.

Owners would retain voting control over the business and all outside investors would be subject to a buyout option. Such an option would guarantee to the investor a return on investment over the investment period exceeding the annual average bank interest rate by the same amount as the required annual dividend.

Involved investor participation could be with start-ups (comparable to angel investors) or with expansions (comparable to venture capitalists), but individual investments would be small compared to those of conventional early corporate investors.

This model would require a new sector of the financial

community to facilitate the connection between the population seeking to become involved investors, and the investment opportunities in which they might have an interest.

A small business infrastructure providing effective small business education whose accreditation would be of significance, with access to involved investor funding, would elevate the status of small businesses as investment opportunities. This could ultimately make them an attractive investment area for community banks.

Given these circumstances, a private sector small business financial industry could develop. Risk capital from involved investors packaged with commercial bank loans could become the means to support the growth of a vibrant small business sector.

For skeptics who may see all this as pie in the sky, a small business co-founded by a colleague and myself has been structured in the manner discussed above. It was financed by "involved" outside investors and has created an online small business training center (vtsbtc.com). This is designed to promote the development of the new small business infrastructure described above.

The picture that I have presented in this chapter shows that a new business sector could develop in which a new generation of small businesses facilitated by current and ongoing technological advances, could competitively challenge the dominance of large publicly owned corporations.

The improved motivational atmosphere and more intimate relationships plausible in a small business offer a psychological advantage to its employees. This, extrapolated throughout society, would mean a happier and more productive work force.

Small business owners lack the power acquired by managers in large organizations. This greatly reduces the corrupting temptations to which they are exposed and thus reduces the behavior that promotes the need for government regulation. It also diminishes the abusive use of corporate money in politics. Further, the success of small businesses in becoming competitively more significant will act to reduce the disparity in income that characterizes labor from management in the large business sector.

Pluralism in the economy will increase as small businesses become more dominant. Such pluralism will enhance both the diversity of product availability and price competitiveness. Small businesses facing bankruptcy can quietly disappear with little impact on the economy and certainly without attracting any government bailouts.

The burgeoning of both quality and quantity from the small business sector would not only bring greater responsiveness and plurality to the marketplace but also greater employment stability. Small businesses cannot engage in the draconian layoffs that characterize the large business response to a bottom line squeeze.

All of these factors provide for greater stability in the economy and foster a healthy refocusing on local problem solving. Thus the existence of both competitive reality and social desirability could represent powerful evolutionary forces making possible a dramatic expansion of the small business sector with an appropriate contraction in the importance and significance of the public corporation in shaping the economy. This would be one of the means to help divert us from the "blind canyon" destination toward which our current evolutionary path is inexorably leading.

Chapter VI

*E*ducation

Technological changes affecting the marketplace are making unprecedented demands on the labor force. The ability of people entering the labor force to respond successfully to this rate of change is now seen as intimately connected to the quality of the public school education they receive. This quality is presently seen as inadequate. A long-standing political debate is all about how public school education needs to be reformed to better meet this challenge.

I became involved with public school education shortly after selling my business interests to my children and retiring from my professional activities. My offer was accepted to fill a vacancy on the school board of the elementary school in the small Vermont town where I live.

Vermont is one of the few places where almost every small town in the state has its own elementary school. Some 226 of these each have their own school board. These schools graduate their students to some 51 union district middle and high schools, each with its own school board. This proliferation of local school boards is characteristic of the Vermont spirit of local control. This has been much criticized by the Vermont Department of Education that recently (2015) resulted in legislation designed to ultimately force consolidation.

The stories of my activities as a school board member, however, would never have come about except for this lack of consolidation. Essential to the events I am about to describe are the intimate connections made possible when a school board's focus is entirely concerned with the governance of a single school in one's own town.

Two important events took place at about the time I joined the local school board. The year before, the State of Vermont had passed Act 60. This was a new approach to funding public education based on a complicated redistribution of a statewide property tax. At the same time, statewide student testing was mandated in a local version of the later Federal program known as "no child left behind".

The second event was revealed by the required screening of the population of pre-school children in the community served by our elementary school. This report indicated that seven preschoolers with Down syndrome were then resident in the town. They would be entering the school in a few years. The special education services that would be needed, according to the principal, would require an increase in special education staffing that would produce an exceptionally large and sustained increase in future school budgets. This would translate directly into large increases in the local property tax rate.

Since I was new to the board and had much to learn about the normal routines without being able to contribute very much, I volunteered to look into these two new questions. What would be the impact of Act 60? What could we do to mitigate the impending large increase in special education costs?

Being a research scientist with two interesting questions to consider was a great way to start what were my retirement years. In studying these issues, I quickly recognized that a particular challenge of Act 60 was how best to interpret the new mandated statewide student test data and how to respond to them.

Further, seven Down syndrome children present in one small school with an enrolment of about 140 students represented an enormous concentration in comparison to the national average of one Down Syndrome child in every 800 births – some 40 times greater than the national average.

An in-depth study of the complex manner in which special education is funded in Vermont highlighted a serious flaw made strikingly apparent by the magnitude of this statistical fluke. Seeking a legislative change in the special education funding formula was an obvious and seemingly necessary response if this problem was to be mitigated.

My initial study of these two questions suggested that major undertakings would be required to make an impact. I put together a couple of preliminary proposals and sent them first to the principal with a request for a meeting to discuss these proposals.

Contrary to my expectations, she did not come up with all the reasons why these proposals couldn't be implemented. Rather she began suggesting the tactics that would be needed to activate and support their implementation. Thus began my collaboration with a highly competent and entrepreneurial principal without whose presence in the school none of the events that I am about to describe would have happened.

My concern with the Act 60 statewide testing was the manner in which such results were to be assessed, and the expectations as to how the school I served should respond.

My generation of scientists was the first to benefit from the introduction of computers and the programming capability to execute complex statistical analyses which previously done manually, had been impossibly time consuming. With these new tools the effective analysis of the complex, multi-variable problems that I encountered in the manufacture of pulp and paper became feasible.

My familiarity with the application of these techniques made it obvious to me that a single measurement of student performance for the small sample size represented by any class in our small rural school, would have so great a variance as to offer little of real value. The solution I discussed with the principal was to produce a much-expanded database to include every available objective measurement she could think of related in any way to student performance. She immediately organized this to include such data as teacher report card assessments, student absences, late reports, student gender, and family poverty based on participation in free and reduced cost lunch programs. It further allowed data segregation by teacher and by students in special or remedial education.

For the following six years, spurred on by the principal, I provided an ongoing array of outcome data for her consideration based on an increasing variety of statistical analyses drawn from this rich database.

The final outcome was a basic, annual report that the principal used with the teaching staff as a fundamental tool to direct a consistent quality improvement effort, updated annually. Among other things it tracked the relative performance of every student in the school throughout their residency, in all disciplines. It compared teacher assessments with standardized test assessments for every child in the school. It assessed the trend line of average grade performance over the years, and provided the principal with student comparative performance data segregated by individual teachers. The principal, in collaboration with the teaching staff, used these annual data as the basis for testing out, modifying, or expanding initiatives for improving student performance. The result was that the students in our school gradually moved up in comparative performance on statewide testing relative to students from the other four elementary schools in our supervisory union until they were consistently near or at the top, and also well above the average statewide performance.

* * *

The first step to deal with the looming financial problem that would result with the arrival of seven Down syndrome children in our school was to study just how special education was funded in Vermont. A coherent report was needed to show why the current special education funding formula would produce such a large and disproportionate increase in the property tax rate in our town.

In Vermont, the local property tax paid for 40% of the cost to provide federally mandated special education services to students in local schools. Sixty percent was funded from state and federal sources. Annual data collected and published by the Vermont Department of Education showed that the local cost to fund special education, on a total per-student basis, varied from as little as $100 at some schools to the well over $1,000 estimated as the future cost for our school.

In effect, the existing formula required that we fund more than 10 times the cost for special education compared to the lowest-cost schools simply because of the statistical fluke that found an exceptionally high number of students resident in our town who required high cost special education services.

With the aid of a local state representative our school board distributed this report. A meeting was organized with legislators and representatives from the Department of Education to consider its contents. Promises were made to study this question, and in the meantime to consider a legislative adjustment to specifically address the problem our Board had identified.

When the legislative session ended with no action, I questioned a local senator I had met earlier. He explained that unless the legislature received a proposal as to how the problem could be addressed, they were unlikely to initiate action.

The next step, therefore, was to come up with a proposed solution and to incorporate it in a second report. Our proposal was based on the principle that the total special education cost for the whole state of Vermont should be shared on an equal per-student basis by all towns in the state. This could easily be done by determining the statewide, per student cost of special education; i.e. total special education spending for all schools in the state, divided by the total student population. Local schools would then be assessed an amount equal to 40% (the local contribution) of this state-wide calculated per-student cost multiplied by the number of students in the local school.

Before proceeding, we sent a draft to the Department of Education's Director of Special Education, and arranged a meeting to receive his input. He objected to the proposal because it would mean that schools would no longer have any incentive to ensure that their special education costs didn't escalate, since their allocated cost was unrelated to their actual local special education budget that would remain unchanged, independent of such efforts.

My previous research had found that DOE archives contained an enormous amount of basic data on special education costs. I obtained permission to access these data and proceeded to develop a mathematical model using multiple regression analysis to predict special education spending.

This was based on an analysis of ten years of data for each

of the fifty-one supervisory unions in the state. A final equation statistically determined the local average cost for supervisory unions to deliver special education services by relating it to the number of students in each of the fourteen different special education categories used to classify special education students. This took the form,

$$Y = n1X1 + n2X2 + \dots + n13X13 + n14X14$$

where Y, the dependent variable, is the reported special education cost for any supervisory union; n1, n2, etc, are the number of students in the supervisory union in each of the 14 special education categories; and X1, X2, etc. are the independent variables, the average cost calculated by multiple regression analysis for each special education category.

This analysis showed that 87% of the variation in supervisory union special education costs could be accounted for by this equation. In effect, this "normalization" of special education costs allowed comparative analysis between supervisory unions. Above and below normal (average) spending by supervisory unions could be identified.

By rewarding well below average spending and penalizing well above average spending, the incentives for efficient delivery of services could by this means not only be reintroduced, but also enhanced.

A report containing this proposal for achieving equity in the distribution of special education costs, while offering the above means to introduce meaningful cost containment incentives, was the outcome of these efforts.

With the aid of our local representatives, our school board returned to lobbying as the legislature began its new session. The result was legislation that instructed the DOE to provide within a year and a half, a review of special education funding with recommendations for beneficial changes. Furthermore, 4% of the special education funds distributed by the state were to be set aside to support exceptionally high special education costs such as were projected for the Moretown School, based on rules to be created by the Department of Education.

It seemed we had accomplished our mission – until the DOE published its rules governing how exceptional special education costs were to qualify for state reimbursement. To our astonishment, these reimbursements applied only to districts in which the late arrival of students with special education needs, newly moving into a community, meant that providing such services would not be covered by the school's annual budget, since that budget had been approved prior to the arrival of the new students.

I later discovered that the DOE director of special education was extremely unhappy with the reallocation of 4% of special education funds in the manner specified by the legislature. Consequently, he was also very unhappy with our school board. He therefore arranged to write the rules in such a way as to ensure that very few applicants, including our school, would qualify for the funds. This would ensure that these funds could be returned to their original intended use.

When the required session for public comment on these new rules was scheduled, our school board and principal were the only members of the public in attendance. The result was a heated debate between our school and DOE officials. We made a forceful case to the effect that these rules seriously abused legislative intent; that is, what the legislation was actually intended to accomplish. The department's own attorney was sufficiently concerned by our arguments that he recommended the rules be rewritten.

When the new rules came out it was obvious they were rewritten in such a way that ours would be the only school district that would likely apply for reimbursement. In this way the minimum loss from the 4% set aside would be guaranteed. Although still clearly abusive of legislative intent, for obvious reasons we chose to let things stand.

Later that year, with several Down syndrome children entering the school, we prepared, as part of our budget deliberations, our application for additional special education reimbursements from the state, based on the newly published rules.

We knew that we were persona non grata with the director of special education who was responsible for assessing our application. The board, therefore, asked the principal to include all expenses that could be connected with servicing the Down syndrome students, no matter how unlikely they were to be accepted. In this way, we hoped to provide the opportunity for significant cuts in our request as a means of satisfying the Department's apparent antipathy toward us.

The result was a request for some $80,000 of extra support. We felt confident that $45,000 to $50,000 of this was beyond dispute. But we had failed to appreciate just how much antipathy we had generated. We were notified that $12,000 had been approved for reimbursement.

We prepared a detailed brief which thoroughly documented expenses that were unequivocally, directly connected to the servicing of the special education needs of the Down syndrome students.

We then approached all our senate and house representatives and briefed them on the issue. They then presented our brief to a recently appointed new Commissioner of Education and requested a meeting, to be attended by all our board members and our local representatives.

Surprisingly, there were no special education officials in attendance, only the commissioner and his chief financial officer. The commissioner opened the meeting by introducing his chief financial officer. This officer announced that the department had reviewed the case and that the state would cover 90% of all costs incurred in the delivery of special education services for the Down syndrome students in our school. It was a very brief meeting.

In response to the other instruction from the legislature, the director of special education announced that a special education funding formula work group was to be established. It would develop the report as requested by the legislature. Our board communicated a desire to have a representative on this working group. We then learned from a public announcement that the group was to begin with its initial meeting the next day. Our request had been ignored.

A call was made to our senior senator. He was familiar with our work in this area. He called the director of special education and informed him in no uncertain terms, that we were to be represented on the working group. He then instructed us to send our representative to the scheduled meeting. In this way, I became part of an impressive bureaucratic exercise. I gradually came to realize that it was designed to form a consensus in favor of maintaining the existing special education funding formula with, perhaps, a few minor changes.

The working group included two-dozen special education providers and administrators. Each was well acquainted with the director of special education. He brilliantly facilitated weekly, three-hour sessions over the next two-and-a-half months. I was the only school board member in attendance.

I learned a great deal about the minutia of how special education services were delivered in Vermont, about rules and regulations and reporting requirements. I was given ample opportunity to present the ideas on changes to the funding formula that our board had proposed in the material we developed for our appeals to the legislature.

Toward the end of these sessions, the group was asked to focus its attention on which of three general approaches (one being the approach advanced by our board) would be best able to deliver equity of reimbursement, while promoting cost containment. At the end of the penultimate session, the director called for an informal vote. Almost unanimously the group expressed the view that the existing formula offered the best opportunity to achieve these desired outcomes.

At the final meeting, I asked for a discussion as to the reasoning by which people had reached the conclusions they had expressed at the end of the prior meeting. This proved to be a fascinating discussion, during which the attendees increasingly acknowledged aspects of the proposal that I had championed which they had not fully appreciated. Toward the end of the session, the director intervened, indicating that, since a significant number of the group were absent – which was certainly true – no final recommendation for a particular course of action could be made. His suggestion was that we present the options we had considered and leave any final decision to the commissioner of education. This outcome was to be reported at a scheduled meeting with another newly appointed commissioner.

Having no confidence that the report produced by the director would fairly represent the lack of consensus that had become evident at the last session, I proposed to our board that we should submit our own report, which I would draft. This was agreed to, and led to the final act in this bureaucratic drama – the meeting with the new commissioner.

Many members of the working group were present along with the new commissioner and the director of special education. The director opened the meeting by indicating to the commissioner that the group had worked diligently over several months, explored a number of options, etc. etc., and recommended that the existing formula should be retained but with a number of specific, if minor, changes. I was floored.

After a number of other members were asked to make presentations, the director called on me to comment on the proposal from our board. I rose from my seat with the report our board had prepared, presented it to the commissioner with a terse statement that it contained a complete description, and left the room. Unbeknownst to me the director had called another meeting and convinced the attendees to vote in favor of the plan that he had wanted from the very start.

The new commissioner asked the legislature for a delay in meeting their request for recommendations on special education funding in Vermont, citing his very recent appointment as the reason. This was granted.

Shortly thereafter I left the board. The report to the legislature, if made, never became public. As far as I know, the whole matter was quietly buried. Certainly, the special education funding formula remains unchanged.

The one beneficial consequence of this extended effort was that the Moretown Elementary School did receive the extra state funding from the DOE over the years when the Down syndrome children were resident in the school. The extra funding, in excess of a quarter of a million dollars, if not received, would have required a substantial increase in the local property tax rate.

I have highlighted my school board experiences through the optics of these two projects because they illustrate what can be achieved by the combination of an effective school board and an effective principal working in concert.

While such an occurrence may be unusual, this particular congruence is highly unlikely to have happened in any large multi-school educational grouping. Under such circumstances, no close working relationship between a school board and one particular school principal is likely to occur.

Education happens in classrooms. Each school can thus be conceived as a laboratory in which educational experiments are daily in progress. Delivery of education would not be a national concern if the educational system recognized the fundamental significance of this reality and organized itself accordingly.

When I started on the school board, meetings were held twice a month for 2-3 evening hours and frequently longer than this. In addition to the legal work of the board and the review of special projects, happenings in the daily life of the school were brought forward for discussion. These came from contacts with parents and teachers. Many members of local school boards have children in the same school. This is an important motivation for serving. However, these discussions occupied considerable time.

As I gained experience and my collaboration on the projects outlined earlier built trust with the principal, I queried her about the value to her of such discussions. Although politely phrased, her perception of them as a waste of time was evident.

At a board retreat held after my second year on the board, we discussed ways by which the board could function more efficiently. This led to a proposal that we meet only once a month. Also, meetings would start at 6:30 PM and end at the latest, by 9:00 PM. Further, decision-requiring issues would be atop any agenda. Other topics could then be discussed, but they would flow to the next meeting's agenda once 9 PM arrived.

Following this, the retiring chairman was replaced and I was elected secretary. The new chairman and I began a fruitful collaboration exploring just how a local school board could best function.

Thereafter the board was not only involved in budget development and other legally required activities, and in reviewing and supporting the projects already outlined, but also worked closely with the principal to focus on two issues.

These did not include any day-to-day happenings in the school unless at the request of the principal. Rather they had to do with either improving the quality of education or reducing the cost of delivering it. Central to the former was the student assessment reporting system that I'd worked with the principal to create. One strand of the latter was the effort to alter the special education funding formula.

Thereafter, the last part of most board meetings were occupied with brainstorming ideas related to these two issues. It became an expectation that the board would each year receive from the principal an annual initiative for (a) quality improvement and (b) cost containment.

Over the following years we, in effect, set up the school as a laboratory to annually test out some initiative proposed by the principal to improve educational outcomes and to contain expenditures, as conceived and developed over the course of the prior year.

This worked exceedingly well because we had a principal capable of using this support to gain the enthusiastic involvement of the teaching staff in pursuing both these goals. It is also important to note that in Vermont, local school boards have the legal power to operate in a very independent manner. This is constrained only by the fact that any failure to meet requirements as established by state law could jeopardize state funding.

By way of illustration, in the development of the student assessment system it became desirable to have teachers work toward standardizing the manner in which they made student report card assessments. The principal expressed concern that this new project would make extra time demands on the teachers. The board's response was to ask the principal to identify what other teacher current activities she felt were less important, so these could be replaced. She identified the preparation of student portfolio submissions, required by the DOE, as being done solely for that reason. It was otherwise considered a waste of time.

The board instructed the principal to end this practice and reallocate the time thus created to the new project. If contacted by the DOE, she was to ask them to call the chairman of our board. No such call was ever received.

As a scientist looking back on my school board experiences, I view them as experiments conducted in my search to understand how educational services could most effectively and efficiently be delivered.

When I entered the educational system as a local board

member, much of what was happening made no sense to me. As opportunities arose, I made suggestions that became the experiments that I have described. These validate the feasibility of any school being viewed as a laboratory having the potential for self-improvement through initiatives generated internally.

To expand this "feasibility" into an educational system would require dramatic changes in the way we think about delivering public school education.

The focus in respect to how educational quality improvements and efforts to constrain or reduce costs were to be implemented would shift from the central control of state and federal bureaucracies to the nation's schools and classrooms.

Widely accepted, normalized measurements of each of these two desirable outcomes – educational quality and level of efficiency – would be essential precursors to such a system. Accountability is the necessary flip side of responsibility. But accountability to be meaningful must be in relation to measurements that define how well desirable outcomes are actually being achieved.

The events I have described earlier show how a local school board tackled the question of providing annual student assessment data for the use of the principal and teachers in their school, and how they developed a normalized assessment figure for statewide special education costs. This is strong evidence that establishing meaningful normalized measurements of educational quality, and of the cost-efficiency in the delivery of education, are very achievable goals.

The "no child left behind" standardized test results could provide one of the elements needed in a meaningful educational assessment parameter, but the rest of this top-down management approach would have to be scrapped.

An annual publication, by a DOE, of meaningful normalized measurements of educational quality and of educational costs – presently non-existent – for every school in the state, is an essential requirement. This would allow school board members and their constituencies to properly assess where their local school ranked in terms of average, below average, or above average performance.

Financial incentives could be offered to penalize well below average quality (or above average cost) results, and reward the opposite outcomes. Every school board would then have a clear mission and the ability to focus their efforts far more sharply than is remotely possible today.

State and federal bureaucracies under these circumstances would focus their attention primarily on being effective information disseminators and efficient distributors of educational funding. It would become their responsibility to develop and then upgrade education quality and cost-efficiency parameters and facilitate the manner in which such information was to be made available to the public.

They would be responsible for exploring the successes and failures of what was happening in the schools in their jurisdiction and disseminating such information in an easily accessible and understandable form to school administrators and school board members.

They would, in essence, become the "observers" of the system and focus their attention on ways to support local creativity in the classrooms and support the spread of successful initiatives throughout the schools in their jurisdiction.

On the financing side, these bureaucracies need to ensure that the funding of public education is aligned with this new system, where both authority and accountability have been decentralized and are now associated with individual schools. These schools would also have the freedom, as they pursue the ever-improving outcomes that would be their mandate, to form whatever groupings of schools they believed could assist in achieving these outcome improvements.

What should be clearly recognized is that the public school system so described assesses outcomes using basic measurement in a typically scientific fashion. Non-achieved outcomes are the driving force for new thinking and new experiments. This new system would ensure that progress in improving educational quality and containing costs is an internal feature that requires public funding, receives public oversight, but does not require any bureaucracy to define how it is to function.

This is exactly the manner in which scientific advances are reliably secured. By establishing the school as an autonomous unit, bureaucratic impediments always to be found in large organizations are minimized. Also this design maximizes plurality in the search for more effective educational performance. All of these are the properties described earlier in the book that have been found associated with efficient problem solving. Developing an educational system along the lines described here would represent another means to help shift our evolutionary path away from its present dead-end destination.

Chapter VII

*H*ealth Care

Our survival and collective wellbeing are now determined by how well we organize our societies. This translates into how well we maximize the individual productivity of our citizenry. Individual health is therefore an important public asset. Sick and unhealthy people are not optimally productive. An obvious goal is to help prevent people from becoming sick; that is, to maximize the health of the citizenry.

To accomplish this, accessible health professionals need to be a part of the life of every citizen. Their efforts would seek to minimize the frequency and severity of episodes of poor health in both the short and long term.

This would ensure to every citizen the availability of regular medical check-ups related to the status of their present and future health. It would deliver the advice and incentives to combat behaviors detrimental to health. Furthermore, for periodic episodes of ill health all citizens would have access to individually tailored health care support.

What the above narrative implies is a health "delivery" system, rather than a health "care" system. Health delivery could be considered an investment that by reducing the impacts of individual episodes of low productivity induced by poor health, increases the energy output that contributes to the welfare of the nation. The beneficial consequences for all, that such increased productivity could secure, makes a health delivery system a logical public investment.

The flip side of such an investment, however, is that the productive energies absorbed by a health delivery system should not seriously infringe upon the productive energies available to provide for the other essential needs and desirable wants in society at large. In other words the health delivery system should function at high levels of efficiency.

Health delivery is thus identified as the central focus, with health care as a supportive function. It identifies the public interest aspect that views health delivery as an investment of benefit to society in general. It identifies that efficiency be an essential attribute of a health delivery system.

It should be obvious how alien these attributes are in our current approach. We focus almost exclusively and obsessively with health care as an expense instead of viewing health delivery as an investment. We largely deny the public interest attribute, and we widely acknowledge systemic inefficiencies. Yet we fail to appreciate that these are inherent to and inevitable with the health care models we currently employ.

This preamble is the outcome of another serendipitous life experience. My wife, as a free-lance journalist, interviewed and wrote about the editor of a local, small-town monthly newspaper. This resulted in a budding friendship that in turn led to my meeting the editor's husband, Jepson Wulff.

It turned out that his major preoccupation at that time was drafting a book on his conception of how a health delivery system should be structured. I was intrigued, since his approach neatly fit within the concepts for efficient problem solving that were occupying my own mind; i.e. pluralism, optimization of size, and attributes of the scientific way of thinking. We thus became friends, and the many subsequent discussions between us fathered the preamble and what is to follow.

Jepson graduated from Yale with a doctorate in psychology focused on learning theory. His distinguished career included periods on the faculty of the *Harvard Graduate School of Design*, and of the *Florence Heller School for Advanced Studies in Social Welfare* at Brandeis University.

He co-founded *The Human Ecology Institute*, a non-profit institute for applied research in the design, development, and management of human services and health care organizations. He also co-founded *Learning Services*, a for-profit company that became a leading provider of rehabilitation services for persons with acquired brain injuries. This company rapidly developed ten campuses serving clients nationwide.

These experiences with what he referred to as client-centered systems, and an acute disdain for the current health care system in America, led him to develop and elucidate his own novel ideas for a national health delivery system[3].

3. *A Health Delivery System*
   Self published by J. Jepson Wulff, 2008
   www.healthdeliverysystem.com

I propose to outline these ideas showing how well his health delivery concepts are aligned with the problem-solving concepts that are the subject of this book.

He articulates his goal.

"The concern which is basic here is health. The proposal here is that we replace what we have, with a system which delivers superior health for all Americans, with superior cost effectiveness."

Jepson then stresses that a successful system must establish a satisfactory measurement of the health outcome that the system is designed to deliver. As an example, he suggests the following.

"A perfectly healthy day for me is one when I judge that I am experiencing none of the following: physical distress, sickness, pain, abnormal mental distress, physical or mental disability. I want to avoid degraded ability to perform normal activities. I want to enjoy life every day."

He then illustrates how this can be translated into a scoring system by which anyone can characterize each day with a "zero" for perfect health, a "one" for minor departures, and a "two" for significant departures. The on-going health score is the sum of the daily scores recorded divided by the number of days for which it applies. The lower the cumulative score, the better is the health being enjoyed.

This concept of a measurable health outcome is in accord with scientific thinking; i.e. that a measurement of outcome is an essential ingredient of any proposed solution, absent which no outcome can be satisfactorily judged for its merit.

Jepson then explores the question as to where the responsibility should lie for achieving the health outcomes that the health delivery system is designed to produce.

"I propose that the choice must be the patient's primary physician working in concert with the patient. Only the primary physician can work with the patient to deliver individualized effect and cost containment.

Every consumer in the population served by the health delivery system I am describing must at all times be teamed with a primary physician. This partnership is formed when the patient and primary physician have reached an agreement about how they will interact and what the accountabilities of each will be. In the agreement they recognize that their continuing target is superior individual health, present and future, with cost containment."

As will be seen, this new health delivery system is built around the fundamental concept that primary physicians are to be the responsible entities through which health delivery is to occur. This means long-term, individual patient-physician collaborations. Jepson goes on to describe the nature of this primary physician responsibility.

"The primary physician designs and oversees a continuing individualized program of prevention for each patient and assures that the self-care ability of each patient develops to be the best it can be for that patient. When an episode requires individualized correction beyond the ability of the patient, the primary physician performs diagnosis and plans and provides treatment to achieve best target outcome with contained cost. When an episode requires diagnostic or treatment services by a specialist or treatment in a special environment (such as a hospital) the primary physician continues to be the accountable agent. Thus the primary physician monitors services by specialists and remains accountable for outcome and cost.

The primary physician has the skills needed for contracting with specialist providers selected from a "shelf" of specialists. When monitoring of a specialist provider reveals failure to meet agreed milestones, the primary physician must find a solution such as assistance for the specialist, or replacement of the specialist. The primary physician maintains a comprehensive digitized medical record for each patient in accord with standards. No treatment selected by a primary physician is constrained by limitations set by management of any "financial risk pool" or at any other level in the system."

Jepson sees the primary physician discharging these responsibilities in collaboration with other physicians and support personnel in what he terms a *Health Maintenance Association* (HMA). This is an organization legally defined, owned and operated by the participating primary physicians. Jepson would set a legal limit to the size of these HMAs by establishing some maximum number (e.g. 50,000) of patients to be serviced by any HMA. His logic is that the size should be the minimum necessary to ensure that the statistical distribution of patient health for each HMA will be reasonably close to that of the population as a whole. This ensures a healthy pluralism in the delivery of health services. Again, these features are very much in accord with the ideas for successful problem solving espoused by this book.

"A Health Maintenance Association (HMA) is an association of many primary physicians. It provides a supporting environment in which every primary physician can focus on effect and cost containment one patient at a time. Each physician in an HMA serves a listed set of consumers, each of whom has elected to team with that physician for the long run.

The population to be served by an HMA, as a general rule of thumb, shall be 50,000. Within a state Health Delivery System there is a number of HMAs that can compete with each other for members. An HMA is constituted to serve any resident within the state who chooses to become a member of that HMA – if that HMA is not 'full'. Do not think of an HMA as a building housing many primary physicians. Rather, think of it as many primary physician offices scattered to serve members of the HMA."

Jepson views a state health delivery system as composed of many HMAs. Each HMA is a corporation run by the primary physicians active in its operation. They elect from their group, or elsewhere, the physicians or others who will serve on the board of directors. The board then makes the decisions that determine what services the physicians in their HMA require. These include support services (facilities, nurses, dieticians, etc), and administrative services (receptionist, clerical, IT staff, operational management, etc). The board further decides what reports are to be provided by support staff to convey information as to the success of the operation.

"At the top of the structure of any HMA there are 30 (more or less) primary physicians. No "boss", other primary physician or government agent dictates to any primary physician what services will be prescribed for their patients. The HMA is organized as a corporation. Board members are selected by the practicing physicians in the HMA. The board is empowered to replace any primary physician whose performance, as assessed, is unsatisfactory. The HMA corporation operates a number of services needed to support the practicing physicians. None of these is empowered to manage any primary physician in any way."

Each HMA, as implied earlier, contracts for those specialized services which they decide are uneconomic for them to employ within the HMA itself; e.g. surgeons, hospital facilities, etc. Jepson describes a "shelf" of direct service providers:

"The providers on the Shelf of Service Providers serve all HMAs in the state. The shelf includes all outside direct specialist providers that are available to contract with a primary physician to serve individual teamed patients. Specialist providers on the "shelf" come into play when a primary physician needs skilled assistance in developing a treatment plan or

when a patient needs special services that the primary physician cannot provide. These outside specialist providers, as well as providers of special environments, competitively market their services to primary physicians in terms both of quality of results delivered and charges for services. To select well from among these providers, a primary physician needs to know the historical record of each provider in terms of delivery of outcomes and cost".

What I have so far outlined is Jepson's basic concept that primary physicians working in concert through many independent private companies that they themselves own (Health Maintenance Associations) are collectively to be responsible both for maximizing the health of the nation and for maximizing the efficiency with which such health is delivered. Noteworthy is that this responsibility is accompanied by all decision-making authority as to how these responsibilities are to be discharged.

To make this basic concept work in practice, Jepson visualizes the need for two centralized oversight and support organizations that connect with all HMAs in the state. One is what he calls the *Specification and Assessment Agency*. This agency develops and maintains the central data collection, analysis and assessment capability that provides the "scoring" by which the performance of every HMA, in terms both of the health score of their patients and the cost to deliver this outcome are determined.

Similarly, the outcome and cost of all individualized health care delivered by outside specialist providers with whom

HMAs contract on behalf of their patients, are part of this data mix. This agency ensures that quality of outcome and cost of service for all HMAs and all outside providers is accessible public knowledge. Here, again, we see the presence of scientific thinking ensuring the availability of comprehensive outcome and cost measurement data as the necessary scientific means to promote continuous improvement in performance.

The second centralized organization required in Jepson's scheme is what he calls the *Systems Operation Service*. This organization is primarily concerned with the financing and accounting services that support the statewide health delivery system. This takes us to how Jepson's health delivery system is to be financed. Broadly speaking, Jepson proposes that two distinct "accounts" be authorized for the use of HMAs. One is established by an annual budgeting approach in which all HMAs participate with a budget request to fund the direct services they provide annually. This ultimately results in a common, per-patient funding amount being applied to all HMAs for the upcoming year. That is, a private account accessible to each HMA is funded to meet a per-patient annual budget multiplied by the number of patients being served. This establishes the size of the private account of each HMA that is available to fund the direct services they annually provide.

Accounting procedures and formats established by the *Systems Operation Service* are employed to ensure the *Specification and Assessment Agency* receives standardized cost data. Otherwise HMAs are free to allocate their funding in any manner they wish.

The second account is established based on past years' statistical data gathered by the *Specification and Assessment Agency* for the costs of outside specialist providers contracted by each HMA. This is a general account from which all HMAs in the state can draw to meet their obligations to outside specialist providers or facilities.

The Systems Operation Service reviews and oversees the HMA budgeting process, negotiating to produce the final per-patient funding amount to be used statewide in establishing all HMA private accounts. It is also the body responsible for establishing a statewide budget for the general account that supports the funding of specialist providers.

It further proposes this total budget requirement for approval by the state legislature as part of its annual report on the state of the health delivery system. The legislature decides on how this budget is to be funded.

The Systems Operation Service is the principal vehicle for dynamic, overall integration of the efforts of the health delivery system. This is a support corporation. It is composed of a board of directors and a staff that performs the work to enable the board to live up to its obligations.

The task of setting a schedule for development of the system plan and budget for the next year, and for ensuring its timely progress, is assigned to the *Systems Operations Service*. It sets up the schedule for this process and sees to cooperation and negotiations among functions to meet the schedule. This includes scheduling the drafting of the system plan and budget at all levels. Once the step-wise plan and budget has been completed, the agreed annual budget must be presented to the legislature for orderly negotiation.

The Systems Operations Service is charged with evaluation and reporting on the quality of data provided by the *Specification and Assessment Agency* for relevance, quality and accuracy, and delivering data to the public and to system HMAs. The HMAs have no control over the independent *Specification and Assessment Agency*. They only have access to a review procedure should they question the validity of their performance data.

"A legislature does not have the skills needed to design or operate a health delivery system. Health delivery is based on two technologies: health technology which is largely in the hands of deeply trained physicians; and the technology of design of client centered systems. When we hand controls over our health 'system' to our legislators, we take accountability out of the hands of those who have these skills".

Many details of Jepson's elucidation of his *Health Delivery System* have escaped attention in this broad-brush presentation. Nevertheless the major concepts are now clear.

Jepson sees a health delivery system, paid for by taxpayers, that is designed by systems experts according to a general specification established by the legislature. This requires health delivery be accomplished by on-going, patient-primary physician collaborations in a private system of *Health Maintenance Associations* (corporations) owned and operated by the primary physicians themselves.

The general specification requires that primary doctors in

these HMAs are responsible for contracting with and overseeing any specialist providers as required by their patients and not employed by their HMAs. They do so from a "shelf" of such providers who negotiate service and costs in competition with each other to achieve the revenues they require.

This specification limits the size of HMAs and requires that they report to an oversight organization responsible for the collection, analysis and public reporting of relevant data. These published data monitor the health performance and costs of HMAs and also of the outside providers as contracted by each HMA. They further develop and implement the planning and budgeting process that establishes the *Health Delivery System's* annual funding request for the approval of the legislature.

An initial requirement to bring such a health delivery system into existence would have the state legislature fund a development project. A selected group of system experts in consultation with primary and other physicians, adhering to the principles set forth by Jepson, would propose legislation setting the boundary conditions within which a publicly funded health delivery system could develop.

This would lead to the funding of the equivalent of Jepson's *Systems Operation Service* to develop a pilot program to establish one HMA, and develop the data collection, analysis and budgeting routines needed to service a future statewide health delivery system. This embryo approach could ultimately expand into the statewide health delivery system.

HMAs competing for customers based on publicly available

performance data, will give incentive for HMAs to upgrade the quality of the patient outcomes they deliver. Only in this way can they assure maximizing revenue growth by achieving and maintaining the allowable customer base.

The private accounts of HMAs established by the budgeting process of negotiations, means that the HMA owners (the primary physicians) have great incentive to maximize efficiencies. Greater efficiency will increase the discretionary funds available for their salaries, bonuses or any development projects they may wish to fund.

Outside specialist providers achieve their revenues by successfully contracting with primary physicians as customers, in competition with other outside providers. Both price and quality of outcome data on all outside specialty providers are publicly available. This means that specialist providers have incentive to improve the services that ensure best outcomes and maintain pricing at competitive levels. The rules and budgeting processes developed can include incentives by which those HMAs with the most successful cost/outcome results from specialty providers receive some monetary benefit.

Jepson Wulff's *Health Delivery System* is one that would run itself. Built into its structure are the basic incentives for both improving patient health and constraining costs, with great pluralism to ensure ongoing innovation in both areas. Data measurement and reporting systems would ensure the spread of such innovations.

The marketplace, and the rules of engagement defining the *Health Delivery System*, would work spontaneously to constrain costs. Large administrative and paper shuffling costs required for micro-management by insurance companies or politicians are now absent.

It is a single-payer system with a huge difference. Essentially, it creates a special free enterprise sector of the economy with unique rules of engagement that allow a health delivery system to deliver health with cost containment.

The rules of engagement provide incentives comparable to the private economy as a whole. This promotes the innovation and cost containment that ensures economically viable ongoing system improvements. Data measurement and analysis provide the public and the system with the evidence of the quality and cost outcomes for delivering its services. This makes it feasible for the system to be publicly funded by the informed taxpayers of the state, without any political micro-management.

According to the World Health Organization, in 2011 the U.S. per capita expenditure on health care was $8,608 and increasing at nearly 5% annually. Jepson's estimates of $5,000 to $6,000 per person for his health delivery system, if demonstrated, would be astonishing in terms of the current health care debate.

Exhibiting great pluralism, and being continuously assessed by outcome and cost measurements as befits scientific thinking, Jepson's small-scale HMAs are far more likely to achieve a satisfactory and sustainable outcome than anything currently on the political horizon, where none of these attributes are visible.

Chapter VIII

*G*overnance

The grand experiment in American national governance began in 1776 with a high-minded Declaration of Independence. It was given substance by the constitutional convention of 1787 and set in motion with the adoption of this constitution in 1789 by the original 13 states of the new United States of America.

It was successfully launched with the election of the first congress and of George Washington as president. His refusal to serve beyond a second, four-year term was, for those times, an unprecedented voluntary relinquishing of power. This established a maximum two-term tradition for election to the presidency that with the exception of Franklin D. Roosevelt, and now embedded in the constitution, lasts to this day.

This, together with the separation of the powers of government between the administration, the legislature, and the judiciary defines the American form of democracy.

The general belief and adherence to the rule of law is a great strength of this democracy. America's written constitution and the legal framework that has subsequently developed around that constitution have, over the years, reinforced these beliefs and practices. The legitimacy of this framework has been secured by a legal perception of constitutional limitations and protections as determined by the Supreme Court.

This expanding legal bubble has continuously set in place the new rules of the game deemed necessary to accommodate the changing realities that accompanied the growth of the nation and the evolution of societies in general.

This dedication to the law has ensured that individuals in America have been able to pursue their lives, secure that future outcomes of their efforts would be respected in accordance with the laws of the land. This has been an important factor responsible for the growth of the nation to become the world's superpower.

Accompanying this evolution of governance in America has been an ongoing shift in the responsibility for problem solving from an ad hoc basis by individuals and local communities, to a legal approach centered in government legislatures. Attending this has been the much-expanded reach of state and federal jurisdictions.

In other words, we have greatly increased the size of the institutions responsible for societal problem solving; that is, for securing and administering the funding to support ostensibly problem-solving legislation. The result has been to abuse two of the important characteristics I have proposed for effective problem solving. The potential benefits of pluralism have diminished, and the inefficiencies that attend the growth in size of responsible institutions have increased.

Another feature of this expansion of governance has been the growth in importance of the legal system and its many practitioners. They play a dominant role in state and federal legislatures. This has set the tone for the nature of governance in which the updating or creation of laws has become the primary vehicle by which the population, through the election process, seeks to resolve the problems that are perceived to negatively impact their wellbeing. This has put in place an approach to problem solving antithetical to the scientific way of thinking.

A lawyer's responsibility is to best serve the needs of clients. This requires fashioning and delivering arguments that best support the particular "perception" of truth most favorable to the client. Thus, the teaching and training received by lawyers is to understand the laws of the nation as the basis for selecting and delivering the arguments that are most persuasive of a particular perception of truth.

The courtroom is where a random selection of people form juries to listen to the presentations of lawyers, and decide which of two differing perceptions of the truth is most credible and persuasive. The communication skills of the lawyers involved are of great significance to the outcome. Ostensible fact and solicited emotional bias compete for attention and significance in determining outcomes. This is antithetical to scientific thinking.

A scientist's responsibility is to seek the truth as that which cannot be refuted by any currently available contrary and concrete evidence. Thus, the teaching and training received by scientists is to understand the laws of nature that define truth as presently conceived, and to expand this understanding by developing the concrete data that challenges these truths.

The scientist's perception of truth is irrelevant. The only question is whether any such perception can resist the experimental challenges emanating from the scientific community as a whole. The communication skills of the scientist affect his or her public persona, but they are irrelevant to the acceptance of his or her ideas. Only the concrete and irrefutable scientific facts are ultimately relevant.

Thus, we can see that lawyers, by their very training, when addressing the problems of the nation, have much to overcome in moving toward more scientific modes of thought. Modern politics encourages their inclinations to support particular diverse "perceptions" of truth. These have increasingly become ideological "certitudes" immune from any serious questioning by their adherents.

Since lawyers have dominated the growth of the political system and established the modern form by which the nation pursues its governance, it is understandable that scientific thinking is largely absent from the problem solving efforts of the country's legislatures. The result is a patchwork of proposals deemed politically persuasive and set forth with great conviction. Witness the suspicion that attends any candidate who might be seen to have changed his or her mind – to have "flip flopped" on the issues. On the other hand a scientist who cannot change his or her mind, will ultimately forfeit his or her reputation.

All this ensures that no political policy proposal can be viewed in its true light as a "social experiment". Thus it is un-attended by any proposed careful measurement of the out-come by which its merits are to be assessed. This guaran-tees that any outcome is defended by simply claiming that in its absence the outcome would have been worse – a clearly unprovable conjecture. This is a blueprint for disguising the failures that in other fields of activity are carefully analyzed as the means to seek better solutions. Unwillingness to acknowl-edge failure ensures the perpetuation of a highly questionable status quo.

In other words, scientific thinking is virtually absent from the deliberations of government. Adding this to the overly large institutions and the reduced plurality that has attended such growth, it is small wonder that the problems of our society are merely shuffled about rather than being resolved. They are doomed to do so into the indefinite future as long as ideologi-cal conviction ensures that minds cannot be changed.

A further component of this problem is illuminated by the well-known adage that power corrupts, and absolute power corrupts absolutely. The will to power is deeply rooted in the human psyche. It is an important genetic legacy of Darwinian evolution whereby survival and reproduction, for untold millennia, favored the more powerful of each evolving species. In humans, the acquisition of power inevitably leads to self-serving temptations that can corrupt behavior. The greater the power acquired, the more corrupting become the temptations.

By establishing a republic with a popularly elected relatively short-term president, subject to the will of the people, the American form of constitutional government overcame the problems inherent to absolute power.

With industrialization came the rise of large organizations producing new centers of power. The antidote became larger and more powerful governments. The size of organizations has been increasing at an accelerating rate since the Second World War. This growth continues unabated today.

The larger are the organizations that wield power in society, the greater will be the temptations that corrupt behavior. This is true no matter if we speak of people in large corporations, large non-governmental organizations or large government agencies themselves.

The sporadic scandals highlighted when egregious corruption in high places becomes headlines in daily newspapers are merely the peaks in the landscape of smaller abuses of power. These are evidenced daily in the interactions of the general public and of low-level employees with the rigid practices that emanate from large bureaucracies.

Also of significance is the idea given voice by the French economist, François Perroux[4].

4. Perroux F. "The Domination Effect and Modern Economic Theory"
    Social Research, 17(2): 188–206., 1950.

Perroux proposed that political power as expressed in society is associated with a "dominant" revenue. This dominant revenue, although characteristic of the society as a whole, has the political consequence of especially favoring the parts of society directly associated with this dominant revenue.

For instance, in pre-industrial times England's "Corn Laws" favored the landed aristocracy. These laws protected the source of their rents, the dominant revenue of that period, from the competition of cheaper foodstuffs from the continent.

With industrialization, the dominant revenue shifted from the rents of landowners to the profits of industrialists. Thus came the abolition of the Corn Laws facilitating trade and allowing the workers of the new factories to subsist at a lower cost. Both factors supported the profits of mill owners.

Large corporations now benefit in the same manner. Government legislation supports their foreign sales, or protects their domestic sales from foreign competition, or provides them with tax-breaks for a variety of their activities.

The past generation has seen the rise in importance of the financial sector. It has become a new dominant revenue. Recent government bailouts of this sector of the economy is the latest substantiation of Peroux's theory of the political power of those responsible for the dominant revenue.

These factors combine to support the need for a dramatic rethinking of governance. We need to recognize that governance, as it exists today, is a natural response to factors that were highly significant in the past. They are far less so today.

The world has been transformed since the current forms of governance were set in place. We badly need to reconsider the extent to which today's forms of governance may be vestigial – relevant in a world that no longer persists but ineffective and lacking relevance in the world we have become.

This means seeing ourselves as members of the human species as well as citizens of a nation. Our survival and future wellbeing are now much dependent on how well we organize our societies to maximize the likelihood that we will continue into the indefinite future not only as successful nations, but also, through coordinated efforts, ensure the ongoing evolutionary success of our species.

We need to be reminded that the forces of nature inexorably proceed, adjusting continuously to the inevitable changes, from whatever sources, that the passage of time produces. They do so in the absence of any awareness of the life forms that may exist or may cease to exist on its surface. In our small part of the universe, planet earth doesn't care what may or may not be happening on its outer skin. It simply accommodates to the chemical and physical changes that time brings forth, seeking always to restore the equilibrium to which, science informs, all such processes inexorably proceed.

When our sun begins to expand prior to its ultimate explosive ending, our survival as a species on planet earth will end. That our extinction not happen sooner, for other reasons, is a requirement if humanity, by carrying our species to some younger planet in the galaxy, is to outlive planet earth.

As a species, we today are organized through historical circumstances into independent nations unequally dividing up the landmass of the planet. We give primacy in our governance to the concept of nation. The most important and the most powerful of the governing bodies throughout the world today are, without exception, the national governments of each and every nation on the earth; i.e. not local, not regional, not supra-national.

The evidence is pretty clear that this basic form of governance isn't working very well in respect to our wellbeing as residents of nations or as members of a common species.

Each nation's governing principle is based not on the interests of the species, but at best, on the perceived interests of the fractional part of the species resident within each nation. It is frequently conceived that each nation is in competition with all or many others to secure its own wellbeing; that someone else's gain is necessarily their loss. No legitimate authority speaks for the species itself.

The thought process to better governance requires an attribute of scientific thinking – a willingness to disbelieve, to accept the evidence and see modern governance as seriously flawed – to consider that it must be rethought from a new perspective.

A good starting point is to approach the question of restructuring governance by seeking to incorporate into the thought process the ideas for good problem solving – maximizing pluralism, minimizing scale, and focusing on the attributes of scientific thinking.

The former two attributes force our thinking to focus on local governance. Only in that way can the virtues of pluralism and reduced scale be significantly tapped. By this logic the importance of local governance must be enhanced by greatly increasing its problem solving responsibilities and authority.

This is not illogical, since most problems that we currently address as state or national problems have a significant local content. Poor people live locally. Children are educated locally. People are unhealthy or become sick locally. Environmental problems exist locally. Economic activity is carried out locally. It is conceptually feasible to expect that local governance could acquire some definable responsibilities for developing solutions to problems that are locally experienced in all these domains of human activity. One can conceive problem solving efforts in any of these areas to be initiated by local governance within flexible boundary conditions that evolve and are ultimately coordinated by state governance.

This would ultimately support extensions of governance responsibilities from local to regional to state and then to federal jurisdictions as would best support the quality and efficiency by which identified problems can be resolved.

In other words, governance starts by maximizing the responsibilities and authority first at a local jurisdiction, and then gradually flowing upward through regional and state governance, arriving finally within federal jurisdiction. Each shift in problem solving up this governance pyramid would be undertaken only when the ability, quality or efficiency of problem solving at a lower level is conceptually, practically or demonstrably unsuitable, but not arbitrarily based on untested assumptions or political presumptions.

Finally, in some way, a governing authority must come to represent the final step beyond national governance by which those problems negatively affecting human evolution or concerning the survival of our species require authoritative attention. A newly organized supra-national entity is required, with newly defined global responsibilities and the actual authority and power to discharge those responsibilities.

The development of such a tiered structure of governance is inconceivable except by an evolutionary process that begins at the very bottom – at local governance. It is here that individuals within "natural" local communities can begin experiments by which some measure of the responsibilities totally surrendered to higher authority can be taken back.

It is the nature of democracy that, ultimately, the will of the people will be manifest in the governance of the nation. Power will flow downward only if local communities can demonstrate that effective problem solving can in fact be initiated and administered by local governance. The people will vote for those who can demonstrably solve problems.

The low regard expressed for congress these days is one possible incentive for individuals at the local level to consider an option that they themselves could develop solutions to local problems connected to poverty, to health, to schooling, to the environment, or to any other issues that may emerge, rather than wait for senior levels of government to do so.

I referred above to "natural" communities as the basis for

local governance. These are not necessarily recognized legal communities with existing governance responsibilities, although they may well be such.

I have had experiences within two communities where I have lived for substantial periods of my life. These experiences have strongly influenced my practical thinking about governance.

The stories of these experiences is a good lead-in to the final chapter, in which all the experiences related heretofore are brought into focus on the question of what I conceive could be the future evolution of governance.

* * *

Montreal West, located some twelve miles west of Montreal's city center, was founded in the 1890s by the Canadian Pacific Railroad Company. It was established as a small railroad town where executives and senior employees of the company were housed. The town was located at the junction where the east and west branches of the CPR came together on the Island of Montreal. Thus, railroad tracks enfolded the town giving it a particularly cozy geography. Most of the town was contained by these tracks with a small "old town" enclave over the tracks to the south and a "new town" enclave over the tracks to the north.

The westward expansion of Montreal had, by the mid 1960s when I arrived to live in the community, filled the miles of farmland which once separated Montreal West from the core city. Duplex-type housing dominated the approaches to Montreal

West, in sharp contrast to the large, single-family dwellings on the mature, tree-lined streets in the town itself. With only three or four roads connecting the new Montreal to the old Montreal West, the latter remained a separate bedroom community largely surrounded by the now major metropolis of Montreal.

The governing body, a mayor and council members, was originally selected from the resident CPR executives. Over time this selection process came to be handled by a *Citizens' Association.* When I joined the community this group was populated from the town's social "upper-crust", and membership was by invitation only. Property taxes were low compared to other communities on the Island of Montreal. The efficiency of garbage collection and winter snow clearing were the only concerns of residents. The status quo was quite acceptable.

Then, the old infrastructure – water lines and sewage pipes – began to fall apart and required replacement. Also, at this time, the provincial government bailed out a bankrupt City of Montreal by giving it taxing authority over the suburban towns through a new *Montreal Urban Community* (MUC). These events overwhelmed the town as the property tax rate rapidly escalated. The status quo was no longer acceptable, and the governing body – with no electoral tradition or experience – was overwhelmed.

About this time, due to a personal connection with an existing member, I was invited to join the board of the Citizen's Association. I quickly realized that the group was dysfunctional, always facing difficulties even attracting a quorum for its meetings. I kept a low profile, but was a conspicuous volunteer to help out with any agreed-upon initiatives. After a year, this led to my being asked to assume the role as president, which I accepted.

I immediately put pressure on members of the board who had failed to regularly attend meetings. Most of these were only too pleased to resign. I then talked to a number of people I had come to know in the community about joining the board, with the idea of revitalizing the organization. This led to a major change in board membership with a majority now supporting a rejuvenation agenda.

Amendments to the by-laws were proposed which required that all board members be elected, rather than appointed. Furthermore, it became the responsibility of the board to ensure that at least two nominees were offered for election annually as president, and that six nominees be offered for the four, three-year board membership positions also elected annually.

The role of the Association was also changed from selecting a slate for the election of mayor and council members to encouraging and supporting all nominees that might choose to run for any position; that is, to promote competitive elections.

With the successful adoption of these by-laws, with actual elections determining board membership and the association president, meetings rarely had member absentees. An interesting transition period began for the town of Montreal West.

The above organizational changes soured the past, close connection between the Citizens' Association and the town council. Events then shattered this connection entirely. The town council proposed as the means to mitigate the escalating tax rate, to increase the tax base by building a high-rise apartment on town-owned land, a small park adjacent to the town hall. In its new role, the Citizens' Association brought the issue to the attention of the town through public meetings at which pros and cons were discussed.

The town council had authorized the development of a complete architectural plan in the isolated quiet of its own council chambers. This was revealed only when the completed architectural plan for the high-rise apartment was ready and a change in the zoning law was needed to accommodate construction. The public discussion quickly developed a strong opposition. The subsequent election overwhelmingly voted it down. From the perspective of the town council, the Citizens' Association was to blame for this humiliating defeat.

For the following two years, the association worked hard to activate the community to build some social infrastructure that could be used by the town council, such as Citizen Association committees, to explore solutions for the increasing number of problems affecting the community. This was hard slogging. Meetings set up were poorly attended, and the town council remained aloof to these efforts.

The breakthrough came during my third term as president. The failures of the past years led us to the idea of creating an unusual community day. It was scheduled for a Saturday in October, and the community was invited to a day-long opportunity to explore the "labyrinth."

We made up and arranged theatre flats to create a labyrinth in a large open room in the town hall. Within this labyrinth were a series of manned displays, each with a focus on a particular, desirable community project that had been studied over the past years. Each solicited the involvement of interested citizens. The layout ensured that each display area was a private part of the labyrinth "discovered" sequentially as one entered and followed a tortuous path before exiting.

We built a number of two sided sandwich boards each with a different message promoting the labyrinth, with time and place identified. Volunteers then moved these billboards to new locations throughout the town each day for the two weeks preceding the event. We were determined that this time everyone in the community would be aware of this event and, hopefully, would be intrigued by the publicity.

On a delightfully crisp and sunny fall day our hard work was rewarded. All day, I welcomed a steady stream of citizens with an explanation that carried them into the labyrinth. Even the town councilors and mayor were drawn in. Every display project recruited volunteer energy. It was an amazing day.

A Montreal television team even showed up. When I was drawn away to be interviewed, my precocious ten-year old daughter, who had been observing my welcoming address, took over for me. That evening, my family and I watched the local news on television. The mayor didn't appear in the coverage. I was given a few brief seconds. The rest of the allotted time featured my daughter welcoming visitors.

The project that all of us in the Citizens' Association felt to be of paramount importance was to start a community newspaper. In this way, other community projects could be regularly brought to the attention of the citizenry in an ideal format to support ongoing progress; that is, people could put energy into projects knowing that another group of people would take care of organizing the communication of their work to the citizenry.

The labyrinth experience finally convinced the town council to join our efforts. They agreed to provide some funding to support a community newspaper.

At this time, I left the Citizens' Association, now a viable and stable organization, to take on the task of starting the community newspaper. With the volunteer support provided by the labyrinth, this developed smoothly into an all-volunteer, community newspaper. And so, in 1972 *The Informer*, the Montreal West News and Viewspaper, was launched.

The next milestone was achieved a year or so later when the town election cycle returned. With the help of *The Informer* the Citizens' Association publicized a drive for nominees and assisted those who stepped forward. What followed was the first competitive election for mayor and town council members in the history of Montreal West.

Pre-election publicity in *The Informer* produced a level of interest that made for an exciting election day. Although at first bitterly opposed to the idea of the election as an unnecessary expense, those seeking re-election were mostly successful. They came to appreciate the greater commitment they now felt in discharging their responsibilities.

I left Montreal West shortly thereafter in my move to Vermont. But the transition period I have described continued. Surprising as this might seem, *The Informer* is now (2014) in its 42nd year of continuous publication. It has the same masthead and organizational structure as conceived so many years ago.

The same success in community building that attended my Montreal West years was not achievable when I applied these experiences in my new home in Moretown, Vermont.

* * *

When Benning Wentworth retired as royal governor of New Hampshire in the summer of 1767, he was one of the wealthiest men in New England. An important source of this wealth involved the wilderness country lying to the west across the Connecticut River, now the state of Vermont.

Although both New Hampshire and New York had plausible claims to the territory, Wentworth, on no authority but his own, began granting these lands as townships to groups of private proprietors. These so-called "New Hampshire Grants" established 129 towns in 15 years. Wentworth benefited handsomely from both the £100 fee he collected for each grant and from his practice of reserving 500 acres of the best land in each grant for himself, for later sale.

In making these grants, Wentworth drew arbitrary lines on primitive maps to establish townships, nominally of 40 square miles. He used major rivers as boundaries, but otherwise these towns were formed with no regard for topography. Early pioneers settled in the valleys of Vermont's rugged terrain, where brooks and streams provided for plentiful water both for consumption and for water wheel generation of power.

Thus, when an area geographically identified by Wentworth was incorporated as the township of Moretown, the settlements within these artificial boundaries were widely separated by intervening ridges and streams.

And so it is that, the Moretown, where I have lived for almost 40 years, includes a single village near its southern extremity. Located there are the town elementary school, the town post office, the fire station, the town hall, a general store, and the only significant cluster of homes in the township.

The rest of the Moretown population is to be found in housing scattered along roads mostly leading to much larger communities that border with it. Much of its population, including myself, live closer to larger communities in other towns than to their own administrative center.

Until I became a member of the Moretown Planning Commission, I rarely visited Moretown village. It wasn't until much later, when I joined the Moretown Elementary School Board that I began to think about Moretown as a community.

A somewhat vestigial element of democracy in Vermont is the March Town Meeting, at which town and school budgets are discussed in an open meeting under the variable control of an elected moderator. Citizens, by secret ballot or in open meeting voice or hand votes, modify, approve or reject spending proposals. Since the Moretown school budget represented the largest single property tax demand on its citizenry, upon becoming a school board member, and remembering the importance of *The Informer* in activating my previous community, I went about organizing a second community newspaper. Its name, *Moretown Matters*, was selected in a community vote.

Over a period of four years I integrated my work as a school board member with an effort to reproduce the success I had experienced in Montreal West. Although the paper was well received by parts of the Moretown community, securing the volunteer support necessary to institutionalize the newspaper proved to be an insurmountable task.

One particularly striking piece of evidence illustrated the dilemma. On an annual basis, the elementary school sent a questionnaire home with students, to be filled out by their parents. Of the many interesting questions posed, one asked how well was understood the role of the school board. In spite of the fact that every one of the eight or so annual issues of *Moretown Matters* included an article about school board issues, the response to this question remained unchanged over the four years that the *Moretown Matters* experiment was conducted.

A large percentage of the answers continued to indicate that responders had little to no understanding of school board matters. The final event that underlined the failure of this experiment in community building was the fact that, although my activities and involvement on the Moretown School Board were frequently described in articles published in *Moretown Matters*, after my sixth year, in an election where I had done much to encourage competition, I failed to secure enough votes to continue in office.

* * *

While community building is a feasible starting point for exploring the possibilities of reinventing governance from the bottom up, an important proviso is that such a community must possess the features that establish it as a "natural" community.

Montreal West is a natural community because all its citizens can identify themselves emotionally with the community itself. This is an important reason why community building in Montreal West proved to be successful.

Moretown, on the other hand, is a fractured community. Much of the population identifies emotionally more with the towns that border it, due to their proximity and size, than they do with their own town of residence. Thus, Moretown like some other Vermont towns, is not a "natural" community and therefore is far less susceptible to effective community development.

My experiences therefore highlight the significance and importance of the concept of "natural" communities as the starting point for rethinking the governance of our species. A natural community is easily determined as the residential and work place area whose boundaries would be widely accepted by those who reside and/or work therein. It is important to realize that such boundaries may or may not correspond with those that define current legal community governing entities.

Chapter IX

*E*scaping

Our long evolutionary journey from the very outset – the Big Bang – has been characterized by successive "theme" periods. Each of these periods progressed within the constraints of a particular theme until a breakthrough event occurred. This allowed for a transition to a new theme period, with renewed progress – based on this new theme – leading to another breakthrough event, each one an essential precursor to the next, and so on, down to the present.

After the Big Bang, as currently conceived, a universe of energy expanded for a quarter of a billion years or so, until the temperature fell to a level – the breakthrough event – when matter was first created.

Matter then coalesced into galaxies, with star formation and destruction seeding the universe with an ever-increasing variety of molecules. This theme continued for some eleven billion years.

Then, at least on planet earth, another breakthrough event occurred. Complex carbon-based molecules were created with a self-replicating capability producing the organisms we call "life". So was initiated a new billion-plus year period of Darwinian evolution, eventually achieving the breakthrough event – an organism with a "thinking" brain. Homo Sapiens.

Thus began the evolution of consciousness, an evolution by which our species has progressed in a few hundred thousand years from a simple isolated tribal existence as hunters and gatherers to the complex, globally interconnected, urban living of today.

This has followed the same evolutionary pattern that created our species. The events that have initiated the periodic changes driving the advances in our evolutionary journey as a species, can now be traced to "intellectual" breakthroughs – the new possibilities that accumulated learning have periodically made possible.

We have labeled such periods, the Stone Age, the Bronze Age, the Iron Age, etc. In each case, new knowledge created a driving force that altered the patterns of our existence, creating as it were a new evolutionary path of least resistance down which we could most readily proceed. These events were, so to speak, the evolutionary earthquakes that altered the terrain and thereby redirected the rivers of our existence.

The latest and most significant of these events was the "new way of thinking", Francis Bacon's way of describing the beginning of what became in the seventeenth century the scientific revolution. This greatly accelerated the pace of intellectual breakthroughs, initiating the industrial revolution and creating the path of least resistance that has brought us to the world we are now experiencing.

The technological advances that have made possible the communications revolution represent the latest breakthrough; one that presages the beginning of a new evolutionary period. New possibilities are opening up well beyond what is already evident. The conditions of the past few centuries that have determined the path of least resistance by which our economic and governing institutions have been fashioned and now function, are changing.

We now have the technological means to refashion our governing institutions – to make the shift to a new evolutionary path that such technological advances have made possible.

How then might this new evolutionary period allow us to escape from the governance status quo in which we are now mired? How might we move toward something new that will better serve the welfare of each and every one of us not only in our communities and nations, but also as members of a common species? How might we get from here to there, from an old evolutionary path to something new?

Although a top down approach is inconceivable, a bottom-up approach could actually begin. As discussed in the last chapter, citizens of "natural" local communities could become sufficiently disenchanted with the manner in which current governance is functioning to consider how they themselves, in this new evolutionary period, could tackle societal problems directly effecting their own communities. How might this happen? What might a guiding blueprint look like?

My experiences with community development, as described in the last chapter, have led me to conceptualize, as basic to such a blueprint, a number of community structures that need to be introduced or strengthened. These would facilitate the community engagement required to initiate the processes that could slowly shift our evolutionary path of governance in a more favorable direction.

These community structures can be summarized as including a *Community Credit System* – a form of local money creation; appropriate *Community Communication Vehicles*; and a formal structure for community *Problem Solving Action Groups*. Elected community councils will need to accept responsibilities to help organize and promote these institutional aids for expanding local governance.

Here's what this would mean.

Consider the significance and nature of an online local *Community Credit System* (CCS). It would work like this. Every community member could apply for membership in the CCS. This would require them to submit a standard profile, identifying themselves and specifying what they would offer by way of priced products and/or services for sale in the CCS. The result would become an online product and service directory, updatable at any time, available to be consulted by any member of the community. Each new member would receive a private, password-protected, community credit account containing a start-up amount of credits – say 4,000 – on the authority of an elected community administrative council that would be responsible for managing the CCS.

The products and services that would be offered in the CCS directory would largely connect to things that in the past community members have done in relation to hobbies and interests as well as volunteer work within the community. That is, the CCS would allow the exchange of goods and services within the community that currently would generally not be exchanged within the conventional monetary system.

Members would acquire products or services from other members of the CCS by means of a simple and secure online protocol that would transfer credits from a purchaser's account to a seller's account once the transaction had been completed. The local credits being employed in the CCS would exist only as virtual entities. They would have no physical presence, unlike normal money. Although a seller might think in terms of the dollar when assigning prices to goods and services to be offered in the CCS, local credits would have no exchangeable connection with dollars.

Two other features of the proposed CCS are important. First, no CCS account could accumulate more than a certain maximum number of credits – say 5,000 – as established by the elected Community Council. This means that, once an account reached this limit, any further transaction amounts that would normally add to the total would now disappear.

The second important feature is that after some period of inactivity – say 3 months – again at the discretion of the Council, the total in all such accounts would automatically be diminished by say 10%.

Participation in the CCS would thus be on a "use it or lose it" basis. These properties would ensure that its only function would be to encourage and facilitate the exchange of goods and services within the community. Unlike real money it could not serve as a store of value.

For ongoing participation, each user of the CCS would need to ensure their offerings had sustainable customer interest. That is, sufficient people would want what was offered, would find the price acceptable, and would be comfortable with the outcome scoring.

This would be an average number, based on a scale of 1 to 10, updated by each customer at the time of the credit transfer protocol, identifying his or her level of satisfaction. This running average "satisfaction" score would be automatically calculated and updated in the membership profile.

In this way each member could attract sufficient sales to roughly equal their own desire to make purchases. At the same time, the rate of transactions would need to be such that the account would not remain inactive for too long.

Excessive purchases would ultimately diminish the account toward zero at which time further purchases would be barred until sales had refurbished the account.

The CCS, being administered by an elected council, could readily be used to promote community initiatives, creating credits as needed to secure participation in projects of value to the community. That is, the council could offer contracts to be paid in local credits rather than call for volunteers to support such projects.

The CCS, as described, would act to establish a greater sense of community, to expand interactions between community members and thus broaden community relationships.

It would also become an administrative tool promoting involvement in community projects. Its rules of engagement, as described above, should sufficiently isolate it from the main economy so that outside interference in respect to taxation, etc. would be avoided.

The second crucial requirement for community development is to ensure the existence of a vibrant and effective community newspaper, newsletter, journal or what have you, comparable to *The Informer*, and associated with an active web site. This would ensure the opportunities for the ongoing dialogues, information flows and exchanges that are necessary for any natural community to achieve a successful expansion of local governance.

Third, any natural community that seeks the governance challenge that I have proposed in the last chapter would require the means to produce effective local responses to any of society's problems as manifest locally. This would mean establishing official *Problem solving Action* (PSA) Groups.

Such groups would submit proposals for authorization by the elected administrative council. The goal of any such PSA group would be to propose and execute a project designed to affect in some beneficial manner a local manifestation of any societal problem. The entire focus would be on developing initiatives that involved the local community in local projects to be executed by members of the community with the help, if needed, of paid expertise.

These projects would be cognizant of existing relevant "outside" (regional or state financed) support structures that were in place. As much as possible they would integrate with such efforts. However, it would be an expectation that local initiatives would not be dependent or subservient to these existing entities.

Ultimate authority for project execution would lie with each PSA group, through authorization by the elected council. This means that such local initiatives would be community funded. The mandate of any PSA Group would be to come up with ideas for projects that the committee itself, with help from the community at large, would organize and execute.

These would not be lobbying groups pushing some ideological agenda, but action groups to develop and test out feasible ways to actually achieve tangible gains in solving societal problems.

Any person or group of people could apply to the elected council for PSA group status by submitting a report identifying any problem that is manifest locally, and the means whereby community members could help instigate a local impact. These would address some aspect of any widely accepted societal problem: e.g. poverty, drug use, education, health care, environmental degradation, the economy, etc.

In all cases the challenge would be not to seek consensus as to what "others" (e.g. governments) should be doing, but rather to identify projects of sufficient interest to produce the community energy needed to execute them.

That is, the PSA groups would become a home for imaginative people who could create projects that would engage their own energies and bring in supporting energies to advance projects and see how well they worked out.

The working of a PSA group itself is something that would require attention. My own experiences inform that many community groups are to varying degrees, dysfunctional.

Primary reasons for this are that the purpose for having the group is too ambiguous or too broad or too ill defined to allow the focused discussion that can lead to specific and concrete goals. Furthermore, all too frequently members of a group have personal agendas that detract from a wholehearted effort to accomplish a particular outcome. Finally, an absence of problem solving skills plague many groups, resulting in unsatisfactory or ambiguous outcomes.

For these reasons, some structure needs to be introduced. Clear rules need to be formulated as to how PSA groups come to be authorized. Any problem-solving project that one or more community members have thought about and would like to pursue could be proposed as the basis for a PSA group. This proposal would be submitted to the elected Council as a report that would be assessed to determine that the following specific questions were satisfactorily answered.

What is the project goal in terms of duration and outcome?

What measurements are proposed to assess the success or merits of the project? What are the conceivable obstacles to a successful project outcome and how are these to be avoided or overcome? What resources are needed in terms of support people, community credits and actual money? How is the project to be structured to organize and handle these resources? How and when is the project to be reported to the council? Once the council was satisfied that all these questions had been convincingly thought out, it would authorize and support the implementation of the project.

Finally, these crucial community structures presuppose the existence of an elected body mandated to help initiate, authorize, oversee and support such activities. This is the first step toward reinventing relevant governance at all higher levels.

Many natural communities, as identified by residents, may not themselves be recognized legal communities, but rather a part of some larger legal entity. To become an active, problem solving community, they would need to define boundaries and establish the size and nature of an elected administrative council.

Where a natural community already has a governing structure, it would need to be adjusted or reorganized to accommodate the new responsibilities that expanding local governance would require.

Encouraging new thinking within the community about local PSA groups, just how these will be promoted and then supported and overseen by the elected council, would be an important feature of these new responsibilities.

Setting up, promoting, and then providing the ongoing administration of the new *Community Credit System* would be another responsibility. This would include developing the means by which local credit creation could best support PSA groups.

Another important responsibility of the elected Council would be to develop a fund raising capability that could be tapped to support initiatives coming from any PSA Committee. This would involve the use of credit creation through the CCS; the use of any money generated by taxing authority or otherwise obtained from the community; the solicitation of municipal, state or federal funds as appropriate, and the development of a knowledgeable, grant-seeking capability.

Once active local problem solving began to flourish, two new areas would emerge as additional responsibilities of the elected council. Certain local problems would cross natural community boundaries. These could best be tackled by liaison relationships with adjacent communities. Promoting these would become increasingly important.

Secondly, conflicts could begin to arise as successful local problem solving encroached on existing, top-down services provided by state and/or federal programs. It would then be necessary to introduce the political strength at the local level to begin reordering the political landscape as the success of local governance enhanced its prestige and authority and challenged and replaced elements of the status quo.

An elected administrative council would promote and provide funding support for the activities of PSA groups using a community credit system to help fund community involvement. With a web site and communication vehicle in place, widespread discussion and involvement in the selection and execution of problem solving initiatives would be facilitated.

By these means, any natural community could realistically become an incubator for testing out local problem solving in all areas where community interest and support could be generated. Once communities accepted and expanded this concept of local governance, they would also begin to develop a local "voice" in matters for which there is a logical extension of local concern.

This could affect the allocation of their tax money by state and federal jurisdictions in respect to problems about which they increasingly would have knowledgeable experience. That is, as effective local problem solving developed, more and more involved people could recognize how ineffective is current state and national governance.

They could begin to create the political structures to support the steps deemed necessary to reorganize state and federal governance to better align with and respond to the superior local problem solving skills and experiences that had been developed.

As community governance expands, in the manner suggested, problem solving skills at the community level should improve. Confidence in this manner of approaching problems could result in an extension of the PSA group concept so that regional PSA groups could develop.

Gradually, the political power of this expanding local energy resource could begin to dictate the approaches taken by state and federal governance. The responsibility of elected representatives could come to be defined by instruction from local and regional PSA groups within their jurisdiction.

Being elected would come, more and more, to depend on how well candidates were perceived as effective conduits, delivering the problem solving ideas that flow from their communities for action at state and federal legislatures.

When the concept of governance within natural local communities increased and became nationally expansive, local experiences and programs could come to be summarized in an online accessible manner.

Successful practices, so broadcast, would have an experienced and knowledgeable audience capable of recognizing merit and itself adopting such practices. Thus best practices could spread far and wide.

Another component of problem solving that could be encouraged and find local community support is to develop projects to help a foreign community escape from poverty. Identifying and connecting with such a foreign community would allow exploration of how local skills and resources could be used to help solve problems that are obstacles to advancing the societal wellbeing of such foreign communities.

This would mean determining how to make the connections with people in the foreign community in order to explore how cooperative efforts could be initiated. This could assist these foreign communities to "learn" their way out of poverty.

Introducing a project of international merit, but at the level of local people directly involved with helping other local people in a foreign country, absent direct supervision from senior levels of government could lead to a better understanding of connections between culturally diverse communities. This should prove beneficial to the wellbeing of our species.

Building these forms of local infrastructure with all the advantages now available through modern communications technology could ultimately transform governance. The most creative problem solvers in society could be attracted to local governance as the preferred place to utilize their talents. Such people could become the primary source of the ideas that would determine the implementation roles of state and federal governments.

These roles would then be focused on achieving the coordination demanded by a majority of local governances as most appropriate to these jurisdictions. That is, the politicians elected to upper levels of government would largely be those supported by the majority of the involved local jurisdictions. They would in effect be committed spokespersons for the views adopted by local communities, and not adherents only to personal or party ideology.

What has been described is a means to introduce to governance the problem solving environments that past experiences inform are most conducive to successful outcomes. That is, encouraging the application of scientific thinking, sustaining a plurality of simultaneous effort, and ensuring a size of organization that is optimum, not excessive, to the accomplishment of any desired societal benefit.

A feasible starting point has been suggested for the expansion of the role of local governance as the means to initiate this new evolutionary path. Local leadership and local people could become the primary source for determining and conducting the societal experiments that could guide our species safely into the next century.

This new evolutionary pathway could provide an opportunity, currently unavailable, to accelerate favorable progress toward the sustainable wellbeing of our species and to avoid events that threaten its survival. It could be the means of escaping the evolutionary dead-end toward which we now seem committed.

Epilogue

The nature of the scientific career I chose to pursue meant that earning my livelihood depended not only on my developing "new" ideas, but further required that I successfully "sell" their merits in the industrial market place. This latter requirement, I soon discovered, was a far greater challenge than the former. While meeting this challenge I came to realize that, in general, people are highly resistant to making the "changes" implied by the acceptance of any new ideas. The status quo is far too ingrained and comfortable. I found this to be true not only for the scientific ideas that I promoted as a consultant and the use of the new technology instruments I developed, but also for those problem solving approaches I explored in community activities, some of which I have recounted in this book.

The significance, then, of the basic ideas presented earlier and the future "changes" they imply will no doubt also be widely received with comparable indifference. This epilogue offers a summary that hopefully will challenge skeptics to think more deeply.

The concept of how evolutionary progress occurs is my starting point. As I set forth in the book, such progress has happened slowly in a step-wise manner whereby something "different" periodically comes into existence that triggers a change in the "theme". This change becomes the dominant driving force for the next evolutionary theme period. Since the Big Bang, this progression has produced the advances that made possible the development of our species and now accounts for its ongoing evolution.

The occurrences of such theme changes are, in human terms, rare phenomena. However, scientific knowledge and the historical record inform that they do actually occur. Thus, logically, they will recur into the future. It fits well with contemporary happenings that we could now be experiencing the commencement of just such a theme change.

Appealing to the important scientific attribute – a willingness to disbelieve – suggests the need for a desirable suspension in a belief that current economic and social/political practices are basically sound – a willingness, that is, to consider they actually may be deeply flawed.

The outcomes of current conventional approaches employed in business development and by governments as they seek for the social betterment of their people, have had the unintended consequence of ensuring an economy structured so as to be incapable of fully utilizing the skills and productivity of all its citizens; of failing to inclusively and adequately educate and train all of its citizens to successfully meet the opportunities and challenges offered by a now rapidly changing social milieu; of also failing to provide the efficient medical system that would ensure a maximally healthy and thus maximally productive citizenry. All these outcomes have consequentially deprived far too many citizens of a decent standard of living.

And perhaps most importantly these approaches have totally failed to seriously address in any significant way the truly fundamental questions concerning the evolutionary success of our species, as witness the ravages of global poverty, global internecine warfare, and global environmental degradation.

I suggest in the book that the scientific revolution commencing in the early 17th century initiated a new evolutionary period that continues to this day. Economies of size became the necessary means to exploit the scientific and technical advances of this new theme period. This inevitably produced the structures of modern societies and the nature of their economies, dominated by large corporations and large governments. This "largeness" and much that consequentially became accepted as normal practice in support of this largeness, have led inevitably to a total inability to effectively address the cited defects in our society as observed today.

The spectacular advances in computer-based technologies of the past half century have, through computer programming, transformed business practices and opportunities for scientific enquiry. They have, via the internet, produced worldwide instant communication and via the world-wide-web, at the click of a mouse, provided an infinitude of information on every subject matter imaginable. They are further bringing widespread, inexpensive robotics to the brink of reality. These technical advances collectively represent the "changes" that make possible a new evolutionary theme period. These changes have, at an ever-accelerating pace, been eliminating factors that previously contributed to the logic of "economies of size". This "change" means that largeness is rapidly ceasing to be the necessity that past circumstances demanded.

The transition from largeness to an optimization of size focused on the substantial potential benefits of "smallness" is now conceivable and implied by the book's content and title, *Escaping an Evolutionary Dead-End*.

The main thesis of the book as introduced and supported by the stories presented, is that this transition will see both private and public enterprises come to conduct their affairs by formulating plans explicitly as "experiments". These will be formulated in accordance with the concepts established by the practices emanating from the scientific revolution. That is, they will be based on "scientific thinking" as described in this book. A conspicuous change will be the primacy then given to the proper "measurements" to define planning outcomes as the means to discover whether predicted outcomes are in fact achieved. This will allow the widespread acknowledgement of any failures, currently obscured and suppressed by the lack of any agreed upon outcome measurements. Such acknowledgements will in turn focus attention on the need for rethinking and re-planning rather than perpetuating the consequences of unacknowledged failures, as is currently the norm.

Two additional changes are necessary to accelerate the proposed transition. National and State governments need to discriminate between legitimate legal questions where legislative solutions can be successfully formulated and difficult social problems where efforts should be focused not on legislating ostensible solutions, but rather seeking to create and support environments that will encourage individuals to actively explore societal problem-solving within the local communities where they reside and work. This will introduce the pluralism of effort, which linked with the application of scientific thinking as a norm, will provide the proven means by which to accelerate societal progress.

Secondly the federal government will need to formulate the experiments whereby the money supply feeding the national economy is to be provided directly by the government rather than indirectly by the private banking sector through the fractional reserve system. Only in this way is it conceptually possible for an economy to be able to employ all the skills and productive energy of all its citizenry all of the time.

A final point to stress is that shifting our evolutionary path in the direction suggested in this book is to be initiated largely by the acts of individuals, not by political action through national or state governments.

At any time, individual entrepreneurs can decide to pursue their business development aspirations along the small business path that I have described, rather than the public corporation path. The educational assist to encourage such a decision is already available through a unique online small business training program developed by a colleague and myself and offered by the *Vermont Small Business Training Center* (vtsbtc.com). As the popularity of this new entrepreneurial path increases, a concurrent development will be that of the small business private infrastructure that I have described.

At any time, individual citizens can choose to follow the local community path that I have introduced, to pursue their societal/political aspirations or beliefs. The natural consequence will be a steady improvement in community problem solving, creating a greater degree of community cohesiveness and sense of empowerment. Cumulatively it would change the face of governance to our enormous benefit.

No slogan-chanting crowds seeking to create national consensus are required to set the above scenarios in motion. Individuals functioning in a new way could actually begin a process to remake their societies.

Once started, this could extend the ideals of the American Revolution to not only banish the evils of absolute power but to greatly diminish the influence of power throughout society. This would reduce the corrupting temptations that attend the acquisition of power, and thus diminish the level of corruption in society that has been enhanced by the growth and dominance of "largeness".

We need to stop asking others to solve societies' problems. It will be more effective – and far more fun – for each of us ourselves to locally engage in societal problem solving. From such beginnings, bringing into play the concepts of scientific thinking, pluralism, and minimization of scale, much that will surprise and benefit can be expected. In this manner the transition I describe could be initiated, thus setting us on a path to escape from the evolutionary dead-end that currently confronts us.

Other books published by the author:

Science in the Pulp and Paper Mill
A personal perspective.

Operating a Business
in the Small Business Space

contact
wcowan@wcvt.com

www.ingramcontent.com/pod-product-compliance
Lightning Source LLC
Chambersburg PA
CBHW021423170526
45164CB00001B/76